Getting
Absent Workers
Back
on the Job

Getting
Absent Workers
Back
on the Job

An Analytical Approach

David A. Dilts,
Clarence R. Deitsch,
and **Robert J. Paul**

Quorum Books
Westport, Connecticut · London, England

Library of Congress Cataloging in Publication Data

Dilts, David A.
  Getting absent workers back on the job.

  Bibliography: p.
  Includes index.
  1. Absenteeism (Labor)—United States. I. Deitsch,
Clarence R. II. Paul, Robert J. III. Title.
HD5115.2.U5D55 1985   658.3'14   85-3540
ISBN 0-89930-025-1 (lib. bdg.)

Library of Congress Catalog Card Number: 85-3540
ISBN: 0-89930-025-1

First published in 1985 by Quorum Books

Greenwood Press
A division of Congressional Information Service, Inc.
88 Post Road West, Westport, Connecticut 06881

Printed in the United States of America

10 9 8 7 6 5 4 3 2 1

Copyright Acknowledgments

Grateful acknowledgment is given for permission to use the following:

Figures 2.1 and 2.2 are reprinted by permission from *Labor Relations Handbook—1979*, pp. 514–
515, copyright © 1980 by The Bureau of National Affairs Inc. Washington, D.C.

Figure 2.3 is reprinted (in slightly different form) from the June 1979 issue of *Personnel Administrator*, copyright 1979 The American Society for Personnel Administration, 606 North Washington Street, Alexandria, VA 22314, $30 per year.

Figure 3.2/10.1 is reprinted from the October 1982 *Academy of Management Review* by permission
of Melvin Blumberg and Charles D. Pringle.

Figure 4.1 is adapted from Richard M. Steers and Susan R. Rhodes, "Major Influences on Employee Attendance: A Process Model," *Journal of Applied Psychology*, Vol. 63, No. 4, 1978, p.
393. Copyright 1978 by the American Psychological Association. Adapted by permission of the
authors.

Portions of Chapter 6 appeared in slightly different form in *Business Horizons*. Copyright, 1981,
by the Foundation for the School of Business at Indiana University. Reprinted by permission.

Portions of Chapter 7 appeared in slightly different form in *Prentice-Hall Industrial Relations Guide*,
Service. Copyright 1980 by Prentice-Hall. Reprinted by permission.

Portions of Chapter 9 are reprinted (in slightly different form) from the April 1984 issue of *Personnel Administrator*, copyright 1984 The American Society for Personnel Administration, 606 North
Washington Street, Alexandria, VA 22314, $30 per year.

Contents

Tables and Figures

Preface

Absenteeism is a critical problem in much of American industry, government, and nonproprietary organizations. Management, unions, and employees are concerned with the economic impact of foreign competition and the withering of opportunities within the American economy. The need for increased efficiency is obvious to any observer of the American economic system. The elimination of excessive absenteeism is a necessary first step in achieving a more productive society.

The purpose of this book is to examine the nature, causes, effects, and remedies for excessive absenteeism in the workplace. The discussions that follow are based on what the authors view as the most critical and common causes and effects of absenteeism, and the remedies suggested herein are based on these causes and effects. Naturally, a reliance on the academic literature on absenteeism is obvious throughout the manuscript, but the basic focus is on the practical application of knowledge to the problem of absenteeism.

The analyses and prescriptions offered in this book are applicable to unionized, nonunion, blue collar, and white collar occupations. At certain points of the discussion, attention will be focused on one specific type of occupation, but nonunion managers can benefit from the experiences of unionized firms and vice versa.

As with all projects, there is a multitude of people who deserve mention for their contributions. Our wives and children have had to forego attention that would otherwise have been theirs had this project not been undertaken. To Christina, Margaret, Phyllis, Ariana, Ross, Jordan, Jim, Steve, Mark, Nancy, and Mike, our thanks. Many officers of General Motors Corporation and representatives of the United Auto Workers have contributed greatly to this project. Those whom we have badgered the most and have the greatest debt to are James Pryce, Don Davis, and Richard O'Brien. Marjorie Seib's typing, organizing, and watching after the authors are probably more responsible for this project's completion than any of us realize. Finally, our thanks to our editor,

Lynn Taylor, and her staff for their patience and hard work in putting this manuscript in final book form. Any errors of commission or omission are the responsibility of the authors jointly but are properly placed with Robert J. Paul, whom the other two would have blamed anyway.

D.A.D.
C.R.D.
R.J.P.

Getting
Absent Workers
Back
on the Job

1 Absenteeism: Framework for Analysis, Definition, and Measurement

It so falls out,
That what we have we prize not to the worth
Whiles we enjoy it; but being lacked and lost,
Why, then, we reck the value.

William Shakespeare
Much Ado about Nothing

Shakespeare identified a major problem associated with absenteeism and the formulation of programs to remedy or mitigate its effects, namely, that of recognizing and measuring labor's "worth" before absences occur. As any businessperson or introductory student of business or economics is well aware, labor is essential to any production process, being combined in various proportions with capital, natural resources, and managerial expertise to provide goods and services. Absent labor and the process comes to a screeching halt. The results differ only in degree when individual workers fail to report for work; the non-absentee is underemployed, capital equipment is underutilized, and resources are idled. In short, production is disrupted and consumers inconvenienced. Too often, however, it is only at this juncture that attention is focused on the determination and measurement of the worth of labor—after absenteeism has become a problem.

This book examines absenteeism, its costs, and its causes for the purpose of fashioning an integrative approach toward absenteeism control. As used here, the integrative approach simply requires that the various causes of absenteeism be identified, examined, and considered in the formulation of practical personnel policy. To accomplish this, the authors borrow freely from a great number of different academic disciplines. Primary reliance, however, is on the economics and psychology of work. This emphasis reflects the academic training of the authors and their belief that such an orientation capitalizes on terminology, concepts, and principles already familiar to managers and, therefore, it is more likely to produce positive and sustained results promptly.

Not only is the academic literature treating absenteeism extensive, it is bewildering as well, focusing on very narrow aspects of the problem. While a highly focused approach and the use of sophisticated empirical models and statistical techniques may be appropriate in academic circles, the practical significance of such endeavors, more often than not, escapes the practitioner. The literature appears mysterious and its principles seem inaccessible and incomprehensible to all but the most persevering of academicians. Further, the practitioner is normally interested in the total impact of absenteeism rather than some exotic aspect of the phenomenon. For these reasons, the following analysis of absenteeism and the suggested integrative approach for its control will draw selectively from the economics and psychology disciplines; will be presented in a straightforward fashion, avoiding the use of technical terms and economic jargon; and will focus on the application of available knowledge to the solution of absenteeism-related problems of the workplace—working toward fashioning a practical personnel policy.

SPECIALIZATION AND DIVISION OF LABOR: A FRAMEWORK FOR ANALYSIS

The modern market economy is a complex and dynamic system of interrelated activities. This interdependence of economic effort was understood by Adam Smith as early as the eighteenth century when he wrote:

Observe the accommodation of the most common artificer or day labourer in a civilized and thriving country, and you will perceive that the number of people of whose industry a part, though but a small part, has been employed in procuring him this accommodation, exceeds all computation. The woollen coat, for example, which covers the day-labourer, as coarse and rough as it may appear, is the produce of the joint labour of a great multitude of workmen. The shepard, the sorter of the wool, the wool-comber or carder, the dyer, the scribbler, the spinner, the weaver, the fuller, the dresser, with many others, must all join their different arts in order to complete even this homely production. How many merchants and carriers, besides, must have been employed . . . in transporting the materials from some of those workmen to others who often live in a very distant part of the country! How much commerce and navigation in particular, how many ship-builders, sailors, sail-makers, rope-makers, must have been employed in order to bring together the different drugs made use of by the dyer, which often come from the remotest corners of the world! What a variety of labour too is necessary in order to produce the tools of the meanest of those workmen![1]

Although embryonic in nature, all the important traits of a modern economy were present in Adam Smith's eighteenth-century Scotland. Of particular interest is the division and specialization of labor, which describes the breakdown of a complex production process into a series of simple repetitive tasks. Each worker is assigned but a single task in the process. Smith was unrestrained in his estimate of the division of labor's contribution to economic activity:

The greatest improvement in the productive powers of labour, and the greater part of the skill, dexterity, and judgment with which it is anywhere directed, or applied, seem to have been the effects of the division of labour.[2]

According to Smith, productivity increases accompanying the division of labor could be traced to

three different circumstances; first, to the increase of dexterity in every particular workman; secondly, to the saving of time which is commonly lost in passing from one species of work to another; and lastly, to the invention of a great number of machines which facilitate and abridge labour, and enable one man to do the work of many.[3]

The division and specialization of labor thus paved the way for the development of the mass-production, assembly-line technology that supplanted the cottage industry and skilled-craftsman technology of an earlier era.

Full development of the characteristics of the modern economy would have to await completion of the Industrial Revolution. By the twentieth century, however, few industries remained untouched by the mass-production technology so ably described by Smith in *The Wealth of Nations* two centuries earlier. For example, even construction, an industry long noted for its employment of a high proportion of skilled workers and the absence of traditional assembly lines, has, as a matter of practice, had recourse to commercial construction assembly systems and prefabricated residential houses. Likewise, health care, the last bastion of self-sufficiency and rugged individualism, has succumbed to the specialization and division of labor and the economic interdependence that they beget. The family physician is supported by a battery of nurses, laboratory technicians, administrative staff, and sophisticated equipment. Should the family physician detect an abnormality, the patient is routinely referred to other physicians specialized in the treatment of the particular illness or the affected part of anatomy.

Accompanying specialization has been a veritable explosion in man's storehouse of knowledge and information. Particularly noteworthy have been the gains in the natural sciences, where engineering advances have led to the development of various mechanical, electrical, hydraulic, and other aids to production. Together, mass-production technology and educational advances applied to production have produced a standard of living not even dreamed possible by the most optimistic of futurists in Smith's time—quantities and varieties of goods and services unparalleled in history, yet more time off in one year for the average worker than most workers enjoyed in a lifetime when Smith penned *The Wealth of Nations*. It is not surprising, therefore, that these changes have had an impact on the work ethic and labor supply decision of the average employee. More surprising is the fact that the impact has not been more significant.

THE COSTS OF SPECIALIZATION

This high standard of living has not been achieved without cost. Specialization has produced an extreme degree of economic dependency within and between industries. Just as each work station along an assembly line must be manned for the entire line to produce, so too are plants within a firm or firms within an industry dependent on inputs from other units of production in the same or other industries to operate smoothly and produce at maximum efficiency. Interrupt production at any point along the line and the entire process, backward and forward, is disrupted. Suppliers of the "downed" production unit are denied their usual product outlet (that is, market) and customers of the downed production unit are denied their usual source of supply. Stated somewhat differently, the loss of a single link (for example, the absence of a single worker) in the production chain destroys the entire process. The costs transcend the lost output of the missing link. This contrasts sharply with a self-sufficient, craftsmen-oriented economy, where each employee is a "jack-of-all-tasks," performing all tasks that comprise a complex production process. Here, the absence of one worker entails but the loss of that worker's output. Consequently, control of absenteeism is not as critical as it is in an economy characterized by specialization and division of labor.

Not only is absenteeism more costly in context of a modern, highly specialized, and interdependent economy, it is also more likely to occur. There are two important reasons for this higher propensity toward absenteeism. First, specialization cloaks the individual worker's contribution to the finished product, thereby denying him or her the satisfaction and pride that comes from creative endeavor. Take away a sense of pride, a sense of self-actualization, a sense of self-fulfillment, and the worker soon becomes alienated from the product that he or she helps to produce and from the workplace wherein it is produced. Worker alienation, therefore, is a by-product of the mass-production, assembly-line economy—an economy characterized by specialization and division of labor. More importantly, for our purposes here and as discussed in greater detail elsewhere in this volume, worker alienation is a prime determinant of absenteeism.

A second factor that reinforces the "push" of worker alienation in explaining the higher propensity toward absenteeism in modern, highly specialized, and interdependent economies is the "pull" of a higher standard of living. Specialization-driven increases in productivity can either take the form of fewer hours of work or the form of increased real income. Both tend to promote absenteeism, the former permitting the worker to cultivate a taste for leisure and the latter enabling the worker to purchase additional leisure by taking additional time off as well as the physical means to enjoy it (such as recreational vehicles, boats, and summer homes). So great has the increase in real hourly income been that even the chronic absentee is able to achieve an acceptable standard of living. In short, the products of the highly specialized, technically advanced, modern economy—worker alienation, increased amounts of leisure time, and higher real income levels—have combined to provide powerful incentives to be absent from work.

To be productive, any analysis of the absenteeism problem must be based on the modern economic and social infrastructure, which, if it did not give birth to the problem, certainly provided a fertile environment for its growth. Whereas during the eighteenth and nineteenth centuries, it was mankind's limited mastery of the physical sciences that acted as a constraint on economic growth and development, today it is mankind's inability to motivate and direct the work force effectively that impedes further progress. Quite simply, advances in the natural sciences have been unmatched by advances in the behavioral sciences. Until mankind's understanding of basic behavioral relationships expands and begins to approach its understanding of the natural sciences, further economic growth and development will be notably unspectacular. Although the absenteeism problem reflects but a single dimension of mankind's inability to motivate and direct employees, it is an important one whose solution provides a starting point for understanding and controlling overall workplace behavior. Better human resources management will, in turn, permit society to tap the vast reservoir of production techniques made possible through advances in the natural sciences.

ABSENTEEISM DEFINED

Absenteeism can be defined and measured in a number of different ways. The definition most useful for purposes of this volume is simple and straightforward, namely, "an individual's unavailability for work when work is available for the individual." Absenteeism may be subclassified by cause in a fashion that facilitates analysis of the problem and the formulation of policy.

One such classification scheme is that of J. K. Chadwick-Jones *et al.* (hereinafter referred to as Chadwick-Jones), where absences are either A-Type or B-Type, the former being those absences that are unavoidable in nature while the latter are those that are voluntary—avoidable—in nature.[4] A major drawback of this approach is that the criteria utilized for classifying absences as either A-Type or B-Type will vary with the classifying individual's perceptions of the needs of management and the needs of the work force. As Chadwick-Jones noted:

Where the dividing line between A and B is drawn and what criteria are invoked will depend on individual, group, or situational factors and will produce some differences in attitudes, beliefs, and actions toward individual instances of absence. Ways in which absence is classified will touch on the rights, duties, and behavior of individuals as they relate to the customs, expectations, and practices which prevail in the organization. In some firms a visit to a general practitioner is considered an acceptable excuse for absence, but in others this would not be tolerated. In terms of the work contract, A-Type absences are legitimate and are justified by definitions of necessity. Their determinants may be extra-organizational: for example, disabling and infectious ailments, bereavements, or serious illness in the immediate family, and social duties such as jury service;

or they may be internal: industrial accidents, strikes, suspensions, or lay-offs. The norm of what is a necessary or inevitable absence may be held by individuals or be formed by consensus in work groups; either way it is open to different interpretations.

B-Type absences are those seen to lack imperative personal or situational justification and which allow for the exercise of individual choice and decision. Extreme examples are usually condemned as irresponsible, but such absences too are evaluated by variable standards. Even when criteria for distinguishing A-Type from B-Type absences are agreed upon, acceptable reasons for B-Type absences will range widely.

For example, time off may be sanctioned by employers in a slack period, but not at other times. Wherever such a boundary is placed the principal difference between A-Type and B-Type absence lies in the nature of the cause. Causes of A-Type are explicit, such as sickness, epidemics, industrial disputes; for B-Type the causes are implicit— norms and individual choices.[5]

Despite the somewhat arbitrary classification criteria, the Chadwick-Jones classification scheme does help identify controllable absences, thereby permitting the formulation of policies that better control the behavior of individual employees.

The foregoing analytical framework, however, sheds little light upon the impact that a collective bargaining agreement or any given personnel policy has on overall employee behavior as mirrored by general rates of absenteeism. A more useful classification scheme, one that will be used here, divides absences into the following two mutually exclusive and exhaustive categories:

1. Casual absences. Absences from work that are not authorized by the organization's personnel policy or labor agreement.
2. Authorized absences. Absences from work specifically authorized by the organization's personnel policy or labor agreement and regarded by managers and workers as rights granted to the work force.

Unlike the Chadwick-Jones model, this classification scheme does not rely on *ex post facto* justification of the causes of absence. Instead, the distinction between casual and authorized absences is made on the basis of whether personnel policy or the labor contract authorizes an employee's absence, thus recognizing that many firms and collective-bargaining agreements permit certain types of discretionary employee absences in addition to those that can be justified under the A-/ or B-Type classification system. These absences can either be explicitly authorized by personnel policy or contract provision as an employee right when certain requirements have been met or implicitly authorized by managerial default through lax enforcement of shop rules, failure to assess discipline properly, or inadequate proof that specified standards have not been met for explicit authorization—the absence of just cause for denial of benefits. All other absences are labeled casual even though some may be viewed as justifiable or legitimate.

Absenteeism can be further subdivided by cause (for example, illness, injury, personal reasons). Identification of absence by cause oftentimes reveals that a firm's absenteeism problem stems from one or two major causes. Such a classification scheme, therefore, permits personnel managers to direct limited resources to the elimination of the more important causes of absenteeism.

For purposes of formulating and implementing effective personnel policies and control procedures, the casual/authorized absenteeism system, modified to reflect cause where necessary, is sufficient. Before proceeding too much farther, a word of warning is in order: blue collar absenteeism cannot be effectively controlled without also controlling white collar absenteeism. There is a tendency for managers to overlook the absences of professional and managerial employees because of the difficult measurement problems involved. Yet these white collar employees set the example for their blue collar counterparts. In short, blue collar workers often take their cue from white collar workers, particularly where the latter work in full view of the former. The problem is compounded when managers attempt to conceal it or deny that it exists. In grievance and arbitration proceedings involving the issue of excessive absenteeism, for example, union advocates are quick to capitalize upon any double standard that may exist or duplicitous managerial behavior that may have taken place and argue the elimination or reduction in disciplinary penalties on grounds of disparate (that is, discriminatory) treatment, even though accepted arbitral dogma does not accord such a defense any weight. White collar absenteeism will be touched on again later in this volume.

MEASURES OF ABSENTEEISM

Information and data concerning absenteeism are collected or made available through many sources: the individual firm; businesses formed specifically for the purpose of data collection and publication, such as the Bureau of National Affairs; and various levels of government. The federal government, for example, compiles and makes available on request statistics pertaining to almost every imaginable type of activity, including employee attendance by industry, occupation, race, sex, age, and so on.

Practical use of this reservoir of information on worker attendance, however, is somewhat limited by the absence of a universally accepted, single measure for absenteeism. Indeed, there are almost as many different measures of absenteeism as there are researchers of the topic. The most widely used and accepted of these measures is the time lost index (TLI).[6] Computed as the ratio of time lost to total scheduled work time for some specified period of time (for example, shift, specific day of the week), TLI's usefulness is that it clearly indicates the proportion of each workday or workweek lost to absenteeism. Its usefulness, however, diminishes as the time period over which the ratio is calculated is lengthened. This occurs because longer periods of time are not strictly comparable in terms of the amount of scheduled work time. Hence, the index may generate two different values for two time periods that are in all respects identical (including employee job attendance) save the amount of scheduled work time. Another limitation of TLI is related to that characteristic of the index that makes it an attractive measure of absenteeism: its simplicity. TLI masks or ignores other information vital to the formulation of effective control policies, such as daily variations in the proportion of the workday lost to absenteeism and the number of times an employee was absent during a specific time period. For these reasons, TLI is often used in conjunction with other measures of absenteeism. The most common of these measures are the worst day index (WDI) and frequency index (FI).

The WDI is calculated by finding the average TLI for each day of the workweek over some specified period of time (for example, week, month, quarter, or year, excluding holidays), identifying the best and worst TLIs, and then subtracting the best TLI from the worst TLI. The WDI, therefore, measures the range of variation in time lost to absenteeism. Several variations of this index have evolved, each reflecting the needs of managers to monitor different aspects of the absenteeism problem. The blue Monday index (BMI), for example, measures the variation in time lost between Mondays and Fridays. Other employers have seen fit to develop similar indices that measure variations between workdays immediately preceding and following scheduled days off and some designated ''best day,'' such as the average time lost for the overall period generally excluding the days under examination.

The frequency index measures the total number of absences (that is, the total number of separate instances of absenteeism) during a specified period of time; it ignores the absences' duration. In calculating the FI, for example, a day's absence in the middle of the workweek would be ''counted'' the same as a week's absence—both would constitute a single instance of absenteeism. The FI is primarily used for scheduling absentee replacements to prevent production and service interruptions and for determining the point of excessive absenteeism for purposes of disciplinary action. As was the case with the WDI, managers have modified this basic index to meet special needs. The attitudinal index (AI), for instance, measures the number of single-day absences that cannot be traced to illness, injury, holidays, or vacations. On the assumption that such absences are caused, at least in part, by poor employee work attitudes (for example, frustration), the AI purports to measure employee attitudes toward work. Others have found it useful to compute frequency indices by cause or type of absence (for example, illness, injury, disciplinary layoff, excused, and unexcused), particularly for the evaluation of personnel policies designed to control these kinds of absences.

The discussion up until now has sidestepped the issue of tardiness because much of what has been said regarding absenteeism may also be applied to tardiness—normally considered a less serious form of absenteeism. Formally, tardiness may be defined as an employee's failure to report for work as scheduled. Although disruptive, employee behavior of this type does not entail the loss of an employee's services for an entire workday. For both disciplinary and personnel planning purposes, therefore, managers have found it useful to distinguish between tardiness and full workday absences. Consequently, most employers collect data on both absenteeism and tardiness and construct separate indices thereof. Further comparisons of absenteeism and tardiness will be drawn as need dictates.

SUMMARY AND CONCLUSION

The modern market economy is a complex and dynamic system of interrelated activities. Economic interdependence is the direct result of the division and specialization of labor. This phrase describes the breakdown of a complex production process into a series of simple repetitive tasks. Together with the mass-production, assembly-line technology that it begot and the educational advances in the natural sciences that accompanied it, the division and specialization of labor produced a standard of living undreamed of by previous generations. This high standard of living has not been achieved without cost. In addition to an extreme degree of economic dependency within and between industries that intensifies its disruptive impact, absenteeism is more likely to occur in the modern market economy. There are two important reasons for this higher propensity to be absent from work: the "push" of worker alienation that stems from the routine nature of simple repetitive tasks and loss of worker identity with the completed product and the "pull" provided by the higher standard of living. A higher standard of living may take the form of fewer hours of work and/or the form of increased real income. Both tend to promote absenteeism, the former permitting the worker to cultivate a taste for leisure and the latter enabling the worker to purchase additional leisure as well as the means to enjoy it. Where mankind's limited mastery of the physical sciences constrained economic growth and development during centuries past, today it is mankind's inability to motivate and direct the work force effectively that impedes further progress. Until understanding of basic behavioral relationships expands and begins to approach that in the natural sciences, further gains in economic well-being will be notably unspectacular. An examination of absenteeism and methods for its control provides a starting point for such an endeavor.

Although absenteeism is rather easily defined and classified by categories that reflect managerial concern (for example, casual absences, authorized absences—the classifications that will be used in this volume), no universally accepted, single measure for absenteeism has yet been devised that captures all the different dimensions of the absenteeism problem. Each measure to date focuses on some particular aspect of the absenteeism problem rather than its overall organizational impact. Consequently, practitioners and academicians alike have been forced to rely on a number of different indices (for example, lost time index, worst day index, and frequency index) to measure absenteeism's total impact for purposes of designing, evaluating, and implementing appropriate control policies.

NOTES

1. Adam Smith, *The Wealth of Nations* (New York: Modern Library, 1937), p. 11.

2. Ibid., p. 3.

3. Ibid., p. 7.

4. J. K. Chadwick-Jones, C. A. Brown, and N. Nicholson, "A-Type and B-Type Absence: Empirical Trends for Women Employees," *Occupational Psychology* (1973), 47:75–80.

5. Ibid., p. 75.

6. E. Huse and E. Taylor, "Reliability of Absence Measures," *Journal of Applied Psychology* (1962), 46:159–160.

2 The Extent and Costs of Absenteeism

> When a business man speaks of incurring costs, he has in mind the quantity of productive means required to achieve a certain end; but the associated idea of a sacrifice which his efforts demand is also aroused. In what does this sacrifice consist? What, for example, is the cost to the producer of devoting certain quantities of iron from his supply to the manufacture of some specific product? The sacrifice consists in the exclusion or limitation of possibilities by which other products might have been turned out, had the material not been devoted to one particular product. Our definition in an earlier connection made clear that cost-productive-means are productive agents which are widely scattered and have manifold uses. As such they promise a profitable yield in many directions. But the realization of one of these necessarily involves a loss of all the others. It is this sacrifice that is predicated in the concept of costs. The cost of production or the quantities of cost-productive-means required for a given product and thus withheld from other uses. . . . The businessman comparing the profits of one product with its cost, compares in truth two masses of utility.
>
> Friedrich von Wieser
> *Social Economics*

The cost of absenteeism has many facets that, for the most part, depend on the context and extent of absenteeism experiences throughout the organization, industry, and economy. As the above quotation from the German economist Friedrich von Wieser suggests, the "true" costs of absenteeism may be quite difficult to measure. The direct dollar expenditure for labor that is not supplied or for replacement labor that is not fully employed during periods characterized by low absenteeism rates are easily measured and are labeled explicit costs. On the other hand, implicit costs or costs that are indirect, such as poor employee moral, inexperienced workers assigned as replacements for absentees, and increased control efforts by management are often difficult if not impossible to identify fully and to account for. The result is that often the true costs of ab-

senteeism are understated both by academic researchers and the firm's accounting procedures.

This chapter will focus on the extent and the costs of absenteeism in the U.S.
economy and how organizations may identify and account for these absenteeism costs.

THE EXTENT OF ABSENTEEISM IN THE UNITED STATES

Before proceeding, it is appropriate to ask: Just how serious a problem is
absenteeism for organizations? One way to answer this question is to examine
absenteeism statistics gathered for the U.S. economy. A summary of 1980 data
compiled by the U.S. Department of Labor, Bureau of Labor Statistics, through
both household surveys and workplace surveys, shows that absenteeism is a rather
serious economic problem.[1] For the U.S. economy as a whole, the significance
of the problem can be gauged from the following figures for 1980:

Time Lost to Absenteeism

3.2 percent of all scheduled work hours

90 million hours per week

416 million workdays per year in the U.S.

9 days lost per employee per year (6 days for illness and injury, 3 days for personal and
civic reasons)

1 employee in every 15 is absent at least once a week

These figures translate to the following out-of-pocket, explicit (direct dollar ex-
penditures) costs for absenteeism:

Costs of Absenteeism

8.0 to 26.4 billion dollars per year in the U.S.

66 dollars per day for each day lost to absenteeism

150 dollars for each 1 percent of absenteeism per worker

100 dollars per employee per year

An examination of absenteeism trends across industries as well as over time
underscores the seriousness of the problem presented by the foregoing statistics. The Bureau of National Affairs data, reported in the *Monthly Labor Review*, indicate that (see Tables 2.1 and 2.2):

Younger workers (ages 16–24) and older workers (ages 55 and over) have higher absenteeism rates than other age groups.

Union employees have higher absenteeism rates than do nonunion employees.

Black employees have higher absenteeism rates than do white employees.

Absentecism increases during holiday periods.

Absenteeism has remained relatively constant since 1968.

Larger firms suffer higher absenteeism rates than do smaller firms.

Manufacturing firms have more absenteeism than service firms.

The West Coast has slightly less absenteeism than other areas.

Tables 2.1 through 2.3 clearly show the relative stability of absenteeism rates over time and across industries. Table 2.2 indicates that industries characterized by mass production technology have a higher incidence of absenteeism than do other industries. For example, the incidence rates were 8.5 and 9.1 for union employees in manufacturing and transportation, respectively, whereas they were 7.4 and 4.6, respectively, for their counterparts in professional services and in finance. These data, on the surface, appear to support the hypothesis (noted in Chapter 1) that worker alienation is an important cause of absenteeism.

Figure 2.1 presents much the same information contained in Table 2.2. The data, however, are shown by company size and region of the country as well. Larger companies, particularly those in manufacturing and nonbusiness, have higher inactivity rates than smaller firms, most notably in the finance and industrial group. Although there is little variation in activity rates by region of the country, the north central region and the west have the highest and lowest rates, respectively.

Table 2.4 presents absenteeism incidence and inactivity rates by occupation and sex of the worker. This occupational breakdown indicates that white collar workers, regardless of sex, have significantly lower rates than do blue collar workers. Within the white collar category, managerial employees have the lowest and professional and technical workers the next lowest incidence and inactivity rates—again regardless of the sex of the worker. As for blue collar workers, absenteeism rates are lowest for men employed as skilled workers and women employed as laborers. The major difference in absenteeism rates by sex of the worker, however, is that female rates are differentially higher than male rates across all occupational classifications. The reasons for this will become apparent in the chapters that follow.

TEMPORAL AND CYCLICAL VARIATIONS IN ABSENTEEISM

Even the casual observer of employee absenteeism behavior can detect substantial variations in absenteeism incidence and activity rates by season, day of the week, and phase of the business cycle. Figure 2.2, for example, indicates that late summer and the Christmas holidays are characterized by increased inactivity rates. Although Figure 2.2 presents only 1978–1979 data, examination of the data for years prior to this period led to the same conclusions.

Several studies have also shown weekly variations in absenteeism rates. A

Table 2.1.
Absenteeism Incidence and Inactivity Rates for American Industry by Reason,
May 1973–79

[Numbers in thousands]

Year	Number of workers		Hours		Incidence rate (Percent of workers absent)			Inactivity rate (Percent of time lost)		
	Employed	Absent	Usually worked	Lost	Total	Illness and injury	Miscellaneous reasons	Total	Illness and injury	Miscellaneous reasons
1973	55,283	3,614	2,344,970	81,549	6.5	4.1	2.4	3.5	2.4	1.1
1974	56,248	3,499	2,382,300	79,706	6.2	3.7	2.5	3.3	2.2	1.1
1975	54,700	3,332	2,303,410	78,873	6.1	3.7	2.4	3.4	2.3	1.1
1976	56,414	3,630	2,374,910	82,222	6.4	4.0	2.5	3.5	2.3	1.1
1977	58,422	3,802	2,473,740	87,487	6.5	3.9	2.6	3.5	2.3	1.2
1978	60,153	3,966	2,549,220	89,888	6.6	4.1	2.5	3.5	2.3	1.2
1979	64,810	4,336	2,745,060	94,641	6.7	3.9	2.8	3.4	2.2	1.2

NOTE: Because of rounding, individual items may not equal totals.

Source: Daniel E. Taylor, "Absences From Work Among Full-Time Employees," Monthly Labor Review, March, 1981, Table 1.

Table 2.2.
Absenteeism Incidence and Inactivity Rates for American Industry by Industry and Union Status, May 1978

Industry	Number of Workers (in thousands)		Incidence rate (Percent of Workers Absent)						Inactivity Rate (Percent of Aggregate Time Lost)					
			Total		Illness and Injury		Miscellaneous reasons		Total		Illness and Injury		Miscellaneous reasons	
	Union	Non-union	Union	Non-union	Union	Non-union	Union	Non-union	Union	Non-union	Union	Non-union	Union	Non-union
All industries	18,445	41,708	7.6	6.1	5.1	3.6	2.5	2.5	4.3	3.2	3.0	2.0	1.2	1.2
Goods producing	8,577	13,802	7.9	6.3	5.2	4.0	2.7	2.3	4.6	3.6	3.3	2.4	1.2	1.2
Mining.	268	300	6.0	5.6	4.6	1.4	2.6	4.2	4.2	3.7	2.1	1.0	2.1	4.6
Construction.	1,479	2,402	5.5	5.4	3.6	2.7	1.0	2.7	2.8	3.3	1.8	1.7	0.9	1.6
Manufacturing	6,830	10,020	8.5	6.6	5.6	4.4	2.8	2.2	4.0	3.6	3.7	2.7	1.3	0.9
Durable goods	4,158	6,341	9.3	6.3	6.1	4.4	3.2	1.8	5.3	3.5	3.0	2.8	1.4	0.9
Nondurable goods.	2,372	4,579	6.9	7.0	4.7	4.3	2.2	2.7	4.3	5.8	3.2	2.8	1.0	1.0
Service producing	9,868	27,906	7.4	6.1	4.9	3.4	2.5	2.6	4.0	3.0	2.8	1.8	1.2	1.2
Transportation and utilities	2,575	2,120	7.8	5.7	5.3	3.0	2.5	2.7	5.4	3.8	3.7	2.2	1.7	1.5
Transportation.	1,379	1,062	9.1	5.6	6.0	2.3	3.0	3.3	7.0	3.7	4.6	1.8	2.4	1.9
Public Utilities.	1,196	1,058	6.4	5.8	4.4	3.8	1.0	2.0	3.3	3.9	2.6	2.7	0.8	1.2
Trade	1,360	8,976	6.7	5.3	4.3	2.9	2.4	2.4	3.3	2.6	2.5	1.7	0.9	0.9
Retail.	968	6,579	6.6	6.0	3.9	3.3	2.7	2.7	3.0	2.9	2.0	1.9	1.1	1.0
Wholesale	392	2,397	6.8	3.3	5.3	2.0	1.5	1.3	4.1	1.6	3.8	1.0	0.3	0.6
Finance, insurance and real estate.	275	3,406	4.6	5.3	4.6	2.7	(2)	2.6	1.8	2.9	1.8	1.6	(2)	1.3
Services.	4,002	11,108	7.3	7.0	4.5	4.1	2.8	2.9	3.5	3.3	2.2	2.0	1.3	1.3
Professional.	3,528	7,935	7.4	7.2	4.6	4.4	2.8	2.8	3.4	3.3	2.1	2.0	1.3	1.3
Educational.	2,313	2,526	6.0	6.8	4.3	4.1	2.7	2.6	2.9	3.0	1.5	1.7	1.5	1.3
Medical	967	3,312	9.7	8.4	6.6	5.2	3.1	3.2	4.6	4.1	3.5	2.6	1.1	1.4
Public Administration	1,632	2,210	7.9	5.9	5.9	3.4	2.0	2.5	3.8	2.8	3.2	1.7	0.6	1.0
Federal	810	1,024	8.4	5.7	6.1	3.2	2.3	2.5	4.0	2.3	3.1	1.4	0.9	0.9
Postal	459	68	8.2	(2)	6.8	(2)	(2)	(2)	5.2	(2)	4.4	(2)	0.8	(2)
Other Federal	350	956	8.7	5.5	5.2	2.9	3.5	2.7	2.4	2.0	2.0	1.4	1.0	0.9
State	291	443	8.6	6.1	6.6	4.2	2.0	1.9	4.1	3.4	3.6	2.1	0.5	1.3
Local	530	772	6.7	6.1	5.3	3.2	1.4	2.9	3.3	3.2	3.0	1.2	0.3	1.4

1 All industries and service producing industries include forestry and fisheries and miscellaneous services not shown separately.

2 Rate not shown where base is less than 75,000

Source: Daniel E. Taylor, *Absent Workers and Lost Work Hours, May 1978*, Special Labor Report 229, U.S. Department of Labor, Bureau of Labor Statistics, Appendix A-6.

recent study conducted by General Motors Corporation revealed that while varying somewhat by shift, absenteeism rates peaked on Fridays and Mondays. Studies of other firms and industries, however, indicate a peak in absenteeism rates at mid-week.[2] Few generalizations, therefore, can be made concerning variations in absenteeism rates by the day of the week. With regard to seasonal variations, the late summer peak in absences can be traced to warm weather and the abundance of outside recreational activities, while higher mid-winter rates are due largely to bad weather, illness, and holiday activities.

Absenteeism is also affected by swings in the level of economic activity (that is, the business cycle). Both blue collar and white collar absences vary directly with the business cycle—blue collar more so than white collar because of that category's greater sensitivity to changes in the level of aggregate economic activity. In other words, absenteeism rates decline during recessions when unemployment rates rise and increase during periods of economic expansion when unemployment rates fall. Several factors account for this observed relationship. Probably the most important of these is the fact that the value that employees place on their jobs varies indirectly with the business cycle, becoming greatest

Table 2.3.
Absenteeism Incidence and Inactivity Rates for American Industry by Age, May 1978 and Average May 1976–78

Age	Incidence Rate (Percent of Workers Absent)						Inactivity Rate (Percent of Aggregate Time Lost)					
	Total		Illness and Injury		Miscellaneous reasons		Total		Illness and Injury		Miscellaneous reasons	
	1978	1976-78	1978	1976-78	1978	1976-78	1978	1976-78	1978	1976-78	1978	1976-78
16 years and over . . .	6.6	6.5	4.1	4.0	2.5	2.5	3.5	3.5	2.3	2.3	1.2	1.2
10 to 19 years. . . .	9.5	8.7	4.9	4.2	4.6	4.5	4.3	3.9	2.3	2.0	2.0	2.0
20 to 24 years. . . .	7.7	7.1	4.5	4.1	3.2	3.0	3.7	3.4	2.1	2.0	1.6	1.5
25 to 34 years. . . .	6.4	6.4	3.7	3.7	2.7	2.7	3.3	3.3	1.9	2.0	1.3	1.3
35 to 44 years. . . .	5.8	5.8	3.6	3.6	2.2	2.2	3.3	3.2	2.2	2.2	1.1	1.0
45 to 54 years. . . .	5.9	6.2	4.1	4.2	1.8	2.1	3.3	3.6	2.6	2.7	0.7	1.0
55 to 64 years. . . .	6.9	6.7	4.7	4.7	2.8	2.1	4.3	4.1	3.2	3.2	1.1	0.9
65 years and over . .	7.4	7.7	4.6	4.4	2.8	3.3	4.0	4.6	3.5	3.3	1.5	1.3
16 to 24 years. . . .	8.1	7.5	4.6	4.1	3.5	3.3	3.8	3.5	2.2	2.0	1.7	1.6
25 to 54 years. . . .	6.1	6.2	3.8	3.8	2.3	2.4	3.3	3.4	2.2	2.3	1.1	1.1
55 years and over . .	7.0	6.8	4.7	4.6	2.3	2.2	4.4	4.2	3.2	3.2	1.1	1.0

NOTE: Because of rounding, detail may not equal totals.

'Incidence rate is the frequency index and inactivity rate rate is the lost time index.

Source: Daniel E. Taylor, *Absent Workers and Lost Work Hours, May 1978,* Special Labor Report 229, U.S. Department of Labor, Bureau of Labor Statistics, Appendix A-6.

during periods of recession when jobs are scarce. Absence rates are low during this phase of the business cycle because employees are reluctant to engage in any activity (including absenting oneself from work) that might precipitate job loss.

Traditional seniority arrangements and early retirement programs reinforce the impact that the business cycle has upon absenteeism rates, particularly those of younger and older members of the labor force. "Last hired, first fired" seniority clauses make job security more tenuous than it would otherwise be for younger (and generally less senior) workers during recessions, thereby increasing the value of the job to the worker and thus reducing his or her propensity toward absenteeism. Early retirement programs have the same impact on the absenteeism rates of older workers—in this case, reducing absenteeism during recessions by providing an alternative, namely, early retirement. Originally negotiated in the auto and steel industries as a device to reduce the need for layoffs of blue collar employees, these early retirement programs have been extended to white collar and managerial employees within these industries.

ABSENTEEISM: THE UNITED STATES AND OTHER NATIONS COMPARED

Given the intense pressure of competition in world markets, the absenteeism problems encountered by foreign firms are of significant interest to policy makers, unions, and businessmen alike. Although there exists a natural tendency for people to perceive the "grass being greener on the other side of the fence" regarding labor market conditions, the foreign firm's experience with absenteeism, for the most part, differs little from that of its domestic counterpart. In-

Figure 2.1.
Average Monthly Inactivity Rates, 1979

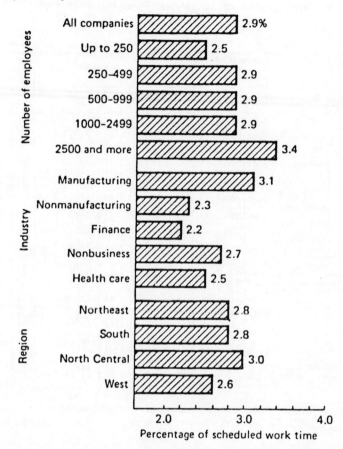

Source: Job Absence and Turnover: 1979, Washington, D.C.: Bureau of National Affairs, 1980. Reprinted by permission from *Labor Relations Yearbook—1979,* pp. 514–515. Copyright © 1980 by The Bureau of National Affairs Inc. Washington, D.C.

deed, one of the most widespread misconceptions concerning foreign labor markets is that workers in other nations such as Germany and Sweden are not absent from work to the extent that American workers are. Table 2.5 should put an end to this misconception. As is readily apparent, the United States compares favorably with all nations except Switzerland and Japan. Neither country is strictly comparable to the United States. Switzerland is a finance, service, and cottage industry economy; in this last regard, much like the U.S. economy before the Industrial Revolution. Japan, on the other hand, is unique in two respects: it has virtually no mining industry and has a much more paternalistic governmental and corporate view of the labor-management relationship. In short, those nations that approximate the U.S. mix of economic activity exhibit ab-

Table 2.4.
Absenteeism Incidence and Inactivity Rates for Full-Time Nonfarm Wage and Salary
Workers by Occupation and Sex, May 1977 and May 1978

Occupation and Sex	Number of workers (in thousands)		Incidence Rate (Percent of workers absent)						Inactivity Rate (Percent of aggregate time lost)					
			Total		Illness and Injury		Miscellaneous reasons		Total		Illness and Injury		Miscellaneous reasons	
	1977	1978	1977	1978	1977	1978	1977	1978	1977	1978	1977	1978	1977	1978
Men.............	36,519	37,464	5.4	5.4	3.3	3.4	2.1	1.9	3.1	3.1	2.1	2.1	1.0	1.0
White collar.....	15,162	15,792	3.9	3.8	2.3	2.3	1.6	1.5	2.1	2.1	1.3	1.3	0.7	0.8
Professional and technical....	5,357	5,876	3.8	4.0	2.0	2.2	1.8	1.8	1.9	2.1	1.1	1.2	0.8	0.9
Managerial.....	5,096	5,218	2.9	2.8	1.9	1.6	1.0	1.2	1.6	1.7	1.1	1.1	0.5	0.6
Sales.........	2,201	2,116	4.3	4.0	2.5	2.5	1.8	1.5	2.3	2.3	1.5	1.7	0.8	0.7
Clerical.......	2,508	2,582	5.9	5.4	3.8	3.8	2.1	1.6	3.2	2.6	2.3	2.0	0.9	0.7
Blue Collar.....	18,631	18,064	6.5	6.4	4.1	4.2	2.4	2.2	4.0	3.8	2.8	2.6	1.2	1.2
Skilled workers...	8,585	8,790	5.7	5.5	3.5	3.6	2.2	1.9	3.4	3.3	2.3	2.2	1.1	1.1
Operatives, except transport....	5,061	5,001	8.3	7.7	5.4	5.0	2.0	2.7	4.9	4.5	3.5	3.0	1.4	1.5
Transport equipment operatives....	2,483	2,377	5.8	6.5	3.7	4.7	2.2	1.8	3.9	4.4	2.6	3.6	1.2	0.9
Laborers, except farm.......	2,502	2,787	6.6	7.0	4.0	4.2	2.6	2.8	4.1	3.6	3.0	2.3	1.1	1.3
Service........	2,725	2,718	6.0	6.8	3.8	4.6	2.2	2.3	3.5	3.7	2.4	2.6	1.1	1.1
Women..........	21,904	22,680	8.4	8.6	4.8	5.1	3.6	3.5	4.3	4.3	2.7	2.8	1.6	1.6
White collar.....	14,617	15,224	6.8	7.5	3.8	4.1	3.0	3.1	3.3	3.6	1.0	2.2	1.4	1.4
Professional and technical....	3,804	4,065	6.6	7.8	3.0	4.6	2.6	5.2	3.0	3.7	1.8	2.2	1.2	1.6
Managerial.....	1,307	1,534	6.3	5.6	3.4	3.2	3.0	2.3	3.0	3.7	1.5	2.4	1.5	1.2
Sales.........	849	881	7.8	9.0	4.9	3.8	3.0	5.2	4.3	4.8	2.8	2.2	1.7	2.6
Clerical.......	8,477	8,741	6.9	7.5	3.7	4.9	3.2	2.9	3.4	3.3	1.9	2.1	1.5	1.2
Blue collar......	4,154	4,336	13.0	11.8	8.2	7.5	4.9	4.3	7.2	6.8	5.1	1.8	2.1	1.9
Skilled Workers...	389	425	9.4	8.6	4.8	6.6	4.6	2.0	3.1	5.4	1.7	1.6	1.4	0.8
Operatives.....	3,514	3,608	13.7	12.6	8.9	8.0	4.0	4.6	7.0	7.3	5.7	5.1	2.2	2.1
Laborers, except farm.......	251	304	9.2	6.3	4.0	2.9	5.2	3.4	3.0	3.0	2.2	1.7	1.7	1.3
Service........	3,133	3,120	9.4	9.0	5.0	5.5	4.4	4.4	4.0	4.8	3.1	3.0	1.8	1.8

Source: Daniel E. Taylor, *Absent Workers and Lost Work Hours, May 1978,* Special Labor Report
    229, U.S. Department of Labor, Bureau of Labor Statistics, Appendix A-5.

senteeism rates three to four times those of the United States—a favorable comparison by anyone's standards.

COSTS OF ABSENTEEISM

The costs of absenteeism may be classified into two general categories: implicit and explicit. Difficult to identify and frequently immeasurable, implicit
costs may be defined as those costs that cannot be expressed accurately in dollar accounting terms. Explicit costs, on the other hand, are generally identifiable and can be expressed in dollar accounting terms. Because of their importance—oftentimes more significant than explicit costs—the implicit costs of absenteeism will be treated at some length before proceeding to the identification
and computation of explicit costs of absenteeism.

Figure 2.2.
Median Inactivity Rates: All Companies

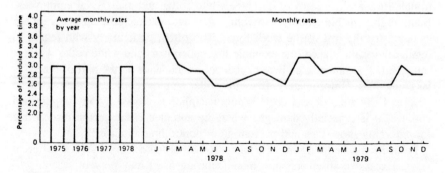

Source: *Job Absence and Turnover: 1979,* Washington, D.C.: Bureau of National Affairs, 1980.
Reprinted by permission from *Labor Relations Yearbook—1979,* pp. 514–515. Copyright © 1980
by The Bureau of National Affairs Inc. Washington, D.C.

Table 2.5.
Median Inactivity Rates for All Industries by Country, 1976–81 (Annual Averages)

Italy	15.1	United States	3.5	Japan	1.5
France	11.0			Switzerland	1.1
Sweden	10.1				
Germany	9.2				

Adapted from: Monthly Labor Review, March 1981, Special Labor Force Reports—Summaries.

Implicit Costs

Managers generally key in on the explicit costs of absenteeism because wages, fringe benefits, and overhead costs are readily identified and easily measured. Accounting costs, however, significantly understate the true costs of absenteeism. Absenteeism affects, in domino fashion, such intangibles as employee morale, discipline, and job satisfaction, which, in turn, increase labor turnover and reduce worker productivity, thereby reducing product quality and making production scheduling more difficult. These events cannot be ignored or separated from other cost elements that comprise the total costs of production. All of these items may be termed implicit costs of absenteeism.

Employee morale and job satisfaction can be affected by absenteeism in several ways. Finding job replacements for absent workers normally requires the shuffling of job assignments. Employees may become disgruntled by frequent shifting from one job to another. This is especially true of situations where workers are shifted to less desirable or unfamiliar assignments. Discipline also may be adversely affected if absent workers are not penalized for their failure to show up for work, particularly when those employees who do come to work are assigned less-desirable jobs. Without appropriate discipline, employees soon learn that they may "come and go" as they please with impunity. Especially troublesome are the cases of absentee white collar and managerial employees. Being highly visible employees, white collar and managerial employees set the example for the rest of the work force. Too often, particularly with regard to regular work attendance, the example that supervisors and white collar workers set is bad. Poor attendance here begets poor attendance on the part of blue collar employees. Unfortunately, few blue collar employees observe the old adage "Do as I say and not as I do." While discipline is eroded by any unpunished absence, it is especially damaged when the absentee is the person responsible for enforcing shop rules and preventing or controlling absences.

Production scheduling may be hampered by absenteeism in several different ways. Excessive absenteeism at manufacturing firms may prevent certain production departments from meeting production targets, thereby crippling, in lock-step fashion, all other departments dependent on them for input. If maintenance personnel are the employees who are absent, repair and maintenance of plant and equipment will deteriorate, resulting in breakdowns that disrupt production. The absence of managerial, production, or quality control personnel necessitates the use of other personnel to "cover" for these absent white collar employees, seriously reducing the efficiency of all affected departments and operations. Replacement workers assigned to production and inspection jobs, especially skilled or semi-skilled positions, generally are poor substitutes for absentee workers. The quality of the work produced and shipped declines accordingly. Management can correct the problems but only by spending a disproportionate amount of time training these replacement workers; only by sacrificing time otherwise best devoted to the pursuit of other managerial functions.

The list of ways in which absences interrupt the production process could be extended for several pages, but the message is clear: absences disrupt production through misapplication and underemployment of productive resources. Managers often have little recourse but to provide for such interruptions either by increasing inventories of intermediate products and work in process, or by use of overtime work in departments hard hit by absences and unable to meet production requirements, both of which are expensive alternatives to effective absenteeism control.

Absenteeism increases labor turnover rates in two ways. First, and most important, increased production costs stemming from excessive absences reduce organizational revenue available for other uses. Simply put, funds utilized to cover the costs of absenteeism—to maintain a replacement labor force, to train replacement workers, to keep an expanded inventory, and to repair machinery—cannot be used for other purposes. The firm's ability to compete—to pay a competitive wage and to ensure adequate job security—is reduced accordingly, thereby providing strong incentives for workers with good attendance records to seek employment elsewhere. Second, the reduced morale, discipline, and job satisfaction that accompany excessive absences also motivate employees to look elsewhere for employment.

Although the discussion of implicit costs has been couched in terms of goods-producing industries, it is no less appropriate to the service sector of the economy. Indeed, there is some evidence that implicit costs are even more significant and pervasive here than in the goods-producing sector. In any case, implicit costs of absenteeism do exist and are substantial, regardless of the industry.

Explicit Costs

Explicit costs of absenteeism fall into one of the following five general categories:

1. *Wage costs*, including overtime premiums and wages and salaries paid to surplus workers who must be hired as replacements in anticipation of absenteeism.

2. *Supplementary benefits*, including benefits paid to absent workers and experience-rated premium costs of such programs as Social Security, Workers' Compensation and Unemployment Compensation.

3. *Costs of administration* associated with recruiting, selection, orientation, and training of the surplus workers required to replace absent workers and the costs of managing absenteeism.

4. *Production inefficiencies* caused by increased labor and material costs due to the use of less-skilled workers to replace absent workers. Also, costs of production delays and the accompanying loss of revenue.

5. *Penalty costs* associated with scheduling difficulties because of absenteeism.[3]

Costs falling within the first three categories are easily measured and conceptually distinct from implicit costs. Although the last two categories contain implicit cost elements, these normally present few problems for purposes of measurement.

COMPUTING ABSENTEEISM'S COST

The cost estimates for absenteeism presented earlier in the chapter are aggregate figures for the economy as a whole. Although interesting, such estimates are not as useful as firm or operational unit-specific estimates. Such "micro" cost estimates can be made by observing the following basic computational steps:[4]

1. *Compute the total number of employee hours lost to absenteeism in a given period of time* (this should include all employees and absences for all reasons except contractually authorized absences).

2. *Compute the weighted average hourly pay rate* for the various employee groups that experienced absenteeism during the period of time studied (this step is used only if the organization pays absent employees during the time they are absent).

Assume that your firm's records show the following data:

Employee Group	Percent of Total Absenteeism	Average Hourly Wage	Weighted Average Hourly Wage	
Factory	80	$10.00	(.80 × $10.00) =	$8.00
Clerical	15	7.50	(.15 × $7.50) =	1.13
Professional	5	15.00	(.05 × $15.00) =	.75
				$9.88

3. *Compute the cost of employee benefits per employee per hour*. This cost can be computed by dividing the total employee benefits cost per employee in a given time period by the hours worked in that period.

   Assume that your firm's benefits per employee are $4,180 per year or $80.00 per week ($4,180 ÷ 52 = $80.00). Therefore, the cost of benefits/employee/hour =

$$\frac{\text{cost of benefits per employee per week}}{\text{hours worked per week}} = \frac{\$80.00}{40.00} = \$2.00$$

4. *Compute the total number of supervisor hours lost to absenteeism in each time period*. This figure can be derived by estimating the average number of hours that supervisors spend on the problems of employee absenteeism each day. The time estimate is multiplied by the number of supervisors and by the number of work days per time period. (Average number of work hours lost per supervisor per day × the total number of supervisors involved with problems of absenteeism × the number of working days in the time period.)

   Assume that each supervisor spends *one-half hour per day* working on problems associated with employee absenteeism; that there are *10 supervisors* who deal with problems of employee absenteeism; and that the total number of working days per year is *240 days*.

   Supervisory hours lost to absenteeism for the year equals one-half hour per supervisor per day × 10 supervisors × 240 days per year = 1,200 total supervisory hours lost to absenteeism per year.

5. *Compute the average hourly compensation (including benefits) for supervisory employees who deal with problems of absenteeism*.

   Assume that your firm's supervisory personnel are compensated as follows:

   average hourly supervisory salary = $12.50
   cost of benefits/supervisor/hour = 2.50
   total compensation/hour = $15.00

6. *Compute all costs associated with employee absenteeism that are not included in the previous steps*. These costs might include overtime premiums, training costs of replacement employees, production slowdowns, and scrap losses because of inexperienced employees. Assume your firm's total cost was, for example, $20,000 per year.

Figure 2.3 summarizes these basic steps and presents sample calculations for each.

Figure 2.3.
Summary of Procedure for Estimating the Cost of Absenteeism

Step	Description			
1	Total employee hours lost to absenteeism per year	28,000		
2	Weighted average hourly pay rate per employee per year		$9.88	
3	Cost of employee benefits per employee per hour		$2.00	
3A	Total compensation lost per hour per absent employee		$11.88	
3B	Total compensation lost when absent employees lose benefits		$9.88	
3C	Total compensation lost to absent employees (Step 1 x Step 3A or 3B)			$332,640.00
4	Total supervisory hours lost on employee absenteeism	1,200		
5	Average hourly supervisory wage (including benefits)		$15.00	
5A	Total supervisory compensation lost on employee absenteeism (Step 4 x Step 5)			$18,000.00
6	All other costs associated with employee absenteeism			$20,000.00
7	Total estimated costs of absenteeism (Step 3C + Step 5A + Step 6)			$370,640.00
8	Total estimated cost of absenteeism per employee per year (Step 7 ÷ 400, total number of employees)			$926.60

Adapted from: Frank E. Kuzmitz, "How Much Is Absenteeism Costing Your Organization?" *Personnel Administrator* (June 1979), 24:31.

THE "RIGHT" AMOUNT OF ABSENTEEISM

What is the "right" amount of absenteeism? From the perspective of the firm that must absorb the substantial costs associated with employee absences, the obvious answer is none. This goal of zero absences, however, is wishful thinking—an unobtainable ideal; a certain amount of time off from work is unavoidable because of illness, injury, and personal or social obligations. Given the inescapable nature of some absences, it is tempting to identify the lowest possible level of absences as the right amount—that absenteeism can never be too low. A figure often mentioned in this regard is 3 percent. Even here, however, there is no unanimity; some managers argue that the absenteeism rate can be too low. Instances often cited as examples include:

1. The employee who continues to work while ill or injured, thereby reducing his or her own current productivity, reducing the current productivity of colleagues by exposing them to the illness, and reducing the long-run productivity of all parties concerned by increasing the probability of an accident with injury or property damage.

2. The employee who returns from an illness or injury too soon, before he or she is completely well, thereby bringing about the same results noted above.

3. The employee who neglects personal or social obligations and activities, thereby harming his or her mental and physical health with a consequent reduction in his or her ability to concentrate. Distraction and stress may reduce productivity as much or more than physical absence. In addition, stress stemming from failure to discharge personal or social commitments is a primary cause of absenteeism.[5]

4. The employee who foregoes periodic absences for purposes of rest and recuperation during periods of extensive use of overtime with a consequent decline in overall long-run productivity. Research indicates that absenteeism is related to the number of hours worked, going up during periods of heavy reliance upon overtime.[6]

What then is the right amount of absenteeism? Although it may appear to be begging the question, the right amount of absenteeism can be defined as the lowest level of absenteeism that does not prompt the employee behavior noted above. This level may vary from firm to firm depending on the specific working characteristics thereof. Firms where working conditions are harsh, for example, may have right levels of absenteeism that are higher than those of firms whose employees work in more pleasant surroundings.

REWARDING ABSENTEEISM

Do firms reward employees for failing to show up for work on a regular basis? As preposterous as this question may appear, recent studies indicate that the compensation programs of some firms encourage and even reward absenteeism.[7] For example, firms whose compensation programs, particularly sick-pay plans, guarantee employees uninterrupted benefits during short periods of absenteeism experience higher rates of absenteeism than do firms that directly tie benefits to hours worked. Stated somewhat differently, absenteeism rates decline where firms condition worker compensation, and continued employment, upon regular attendance.[8] Many firms, therefore, albeit unwittingly and indirectly, not only tolerate or accept but actually reward employee absences. These and related concepts are treated extensively elsewhere in this book.

ABSENTEEISM STATISTICS: MEASUREMENT AND COMPARISON PROBLEMS

No discussion of absenteeism statistics would be complete without at least a brief mention of some of the measurement and comparison problems that limit their use. Some of the most important problems include:[9]

1. *Problems of definition.* There are a large number of definitions of absenteeism. Different studies and companies use different definitions and measures. Consequently, comparisons are difficult.

2. *Problems of data collection.* There is no uniformly accepted classification scheme for collecting and assessing data. This problem is compounded by the fact that firms, more often than not, keep poor absenteeism records.

3. *Problems of validity.* Absenteeism statistics vary markedly with regard to reliability. Few statistics are cross validated. Firms have yet to address this problem.

4. *Problems of data appropriateness.* The amount of multivariate longitudinal data is limited. Most current studies use bivariate correlation models which are, at best, piecemeal approaches. They assume that the variables are related to each other.

5. *Problems of limiting assumptions.* The study of absenteeism has been limited by a number of unduly restrictive assumptions. These include the assumptions that job dissatisfaction represents the primary cause of absenteeism and that employees are generally free to choose whether to go to work.

SUMMARY

Although absenteeism is an extremely important and costly problem for many firms, it is a difficult problem to analyze. A number of different factors account for this: the sheer number of variables influencing absenteeism, the myriad ways in which they interact with one another to encourage or discourage absenteeism, and their sensitivity to a wide variety of different environmental, organizational, and personal characteristics. Coupled with the fact that measurement and control instruments are limited, these factors explain the subjective nature of absenteeism data—that they are subjective estimates at best. Nevertheless, these estimates do shed significant light upon the magnitude and nature of the employee absenteeism problem.

NOTES

1. "Special Labor Force Reports—Summaries," *Monthly Labor Review* (March, 1981), 104:68–70.
2. Steven Markham, Fred Dansereau, Jr., and Joseph A. Alutto, "Female vs. Male Absence Rates: A Temporal Analysis," *Personnel Psychology* (Summer 1982), 35:371–382.

3. Jeffrey Gandz and Alexander Mikalachki, "Absenteeism: Costs and Curves," *The Business Quarterly* (Spring 1980), 45:22–30.

4. Frank E. Kuzmitz, "How Much Is Absenteeism Costing Your Organization?" *Personnel Administrator* (June 1979), 24:29–33.

5. Nina Gupta and Terry Beehr, "Job Stress and Employee Behaviors," *Organizational Behavior and Human Performance* (June 1979), 23:373–387.

6. Nigel Nicholson, Paul Jackson, and Gillian Howes, "Shiftwork and Absence: An Analysis of Temporal Trends," *Journal of Occupational Psychology* (June 1978), 51:127–137.

7. Miriam Rothman, "Can Alternatives to Sick Pay Plans Reduce Absenteeism?" *Personnel Journal* (October 1981), 60:788–790; Clarence R. Deitsch and David A. Dilts, "Getting Absent Workers Back on the Job: The Case of General Motors," *Business Horizons* (September/October 1981), 24:52–58.

8. John F. Baum, "Effectiveness of an Attendance Control Policy in Reducing Chronic Absenteeism," *Personnel Psychology* (Spring 1978), 31:71–81.

9. This section relies heavily on the work of R. T. Mowday, Layman Porter, and Richard Steers, *Employee-Organization Linkages: The Psychology of Commitment, Absenteeism and Turnover* (New York: Academic Press, 1982), pp. 75–106.

3 Theories of Absenteeism: Five Basic Categories

> Pure economics has a remarkable way of producing rabbits out of a hat—
> *a priori* propositions which apparently refer to reality. It is fascinating to
> try to discover how the rabbits got in; for those of us who do not believe
> in magic must be convinced that they got in somehow.
>
> J. R. Hicks
> *Value and Capital*

> Theory is theory and reality is that theory and reality are more often
> strangers than partners.
>
> Unknown philosopher

Absenteeism, like most complex aspects of human behavior, has generated a
large number of explanatory theories, that attempt to apply "knowledge" in a
practical manner to some absenteeism problem. The theories are intended to
account for absences from work and, like all good theories, to permit users to
predict and control future attendance behavior. Although these propositions vary
in their complexity, comprehensiveness, and in their ability to account for absenteeism, it is important to examine them. Current theories borrow heavily from
the research methodology and knowledge acquired from economics, statistics,
psychology, sociology, and labor law, among other disciplines. This body of
information is important because it provides some insight to the behavioral assumptions underlying various theories of absenteeism. It also underscores the
basic fact that absenteeism can occur for a number of reasons and that the phenomenon is influenced by many organizational variables. Unfortunately, interdisciplinary perspectives on absenteeism have been achieved only at significant
cost: the loss or lack of a single, unified and integrated theory of absenteeism.
Simply put, various disciplines utilize their own unique methods of investigation and their own terminology; they analyze different aspects of the problem
and gather information from different environments and at different times; and,
finally, they analyze and interpret their findings differently. As a result, the body

of knowledge concerning absenteeism, although extensive, is a hodgepodge of disjointed, incomplete, overlapping, and sometimes conflicting premises, hypotheses, and theories. Attempts have been made to construct a unified model, but to date they have been only partially successful. Major obstacles to the construction of such a model are that competing theories are not independent nor can they readily accommodate concepts unique yet critical to each.

The current body of knowledge concerning absenteeism suggests grouping various theories into five broad categories.[1] Although some theories and concepts logically fit into two or more of the categories, they are placed in that category that best describes their properties and characteristics. Figure 3.1 depicts these five categories. A brief discussion of each theoretical grouping will help clarify the assumptions upon which the theories contained therein are based and identify appropriate remedies for absenteeism caused thereby. Different theories (that is, explanations and causes) of absenteeism call for different, perhaps unique, remedial actions.

ECONOMIC THEORY

Economic theory is probably the most commonly used explanation of absenteeism. Proponents of this theory usually assume that people do not really like

Figure 3.1.
Theories of Absenteeism: Five Basic Categories

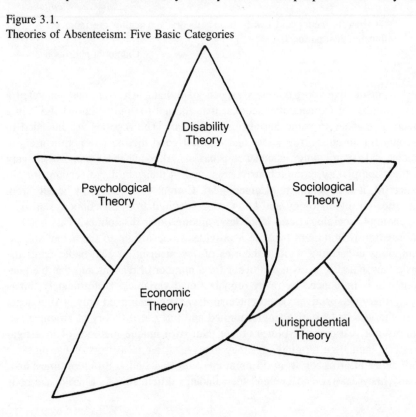

to work; they only work because they have to. At the same time, however, people want to maintain a certain standard of living that requires a specific income level. Holding a job is one acceptable way of obtaining the necessary income. If the income generated by working full time is greater than necessary to achieve and maintain the desired standard of living, the individual simply will not go to work every day. Increases in wages and real income levels, an increase in the number of families with two or more labor force participants, and improved employee benefit plans (which decrease the need for personal savings) are thought to increase employee absenteeism. The argument is that, since it takes less work time to generate the income required to sustain a given standard of living, an individual will work less because he or she does not really like to work in the first place.

PSYCHOLOGICAL THEORY

This category includes a number of theories that focus on withdrawal as a behavioral response to alienation (job dissatisfaction) and need deficiencies. Essentially motivation theories, they can be further subclassified as "passive withdrawal theories" (simple avoidance of the unpleasant situations) and "strategic withdrawal theories" (a means of punishing the organization for the dissatisfaction it causes).

Passive Withdrawal Theories

Inequity Theory

Absenteeism can be viewed as an individual's way of resolving or reacting to a perceived inequity between what they feel they put into the organization and what they get back. Often, a comparison of the ratio of inputs to outputs is made with those of another person. The probability of absence increases with the magnitude of the worker's felt inequity if other ways of reducing the perceived inequity are not available. For example, an employee who feels that he or she does not get appropriate recognition for his or her efforts and achievements may take time off from work to engage in activities where recognition is forthcoming.[2]

Valence Theory

Valence (sometimes called valence/expectancy) explanations of absenteeism refer to the individual's positive and negative attractions toward differing objects and events in the work environment. If the combined positive aspects of the work situation are weak or the negative aspects are strong, absenteeism is more likely to occur. For example, if the pay is good but work content and relations with one's supervisor are unpleasant, absenteeism is more likely to occur than if the opposite is true.[3]

Met Expectations Theory

This theory is a form of cognitive dissonance theory.[4] The met expectations theory can be used to account for some absenteeism. Those subscribing to this theory contend that the discrepancy between what a person encounters on the job by way of positive and negative factors and what he or she expected to encounter may cause that person to be absent from work. In other words, a person who expects an attractive work environment but, instead, finds an un-attractive one may look for more pleasant ways to spend his or her time and may become an absentee problem. This dissonance or discrepancy theory is often combined with the valence theory to explain absentee behavior.[5]

Need for Control Theory

This theory assumes that everyone has a need to influence or control his or her environment. To the extent that a person cannot exercise some degree of control over the work environment, he or she may attempt to satisfy this need through activities other than work. Unable to satisfy the basic need to control one's environment while on the job through regular attendance, these workers look elsewhere—absenting themselves to free their time for other activities (for example, moonlighting, recreational activities, and so on) that will allow such control. This theory contains elements of the "growth need strength" concept.[6]

"I Am Not Needed" Theory

A number of factors can contribute to a feeling on the part of an employee that he or she is not important or needed—that the individual is not essential to the organization. Factors that could contribute to this feeling include the large size of an organization or work group; the lack of observable interest in indi-viduals on the part of management; statements by supervisors such as "you can be replaced"; working on a routine job that can be learned quickly by almost anyone; and the observation by an employee that when someone is absent the work gets done anyway. Any of these factors and others can help to make em-ployees feel that they are not really needed by the organization. When employ-ees feel this way, the decision to be absent is an easy one to make; they believe they will not be missed and, even if they are, management can easily find a temporary replacement.

In most absenteeism cases where this factor is present, it is probably not the primary reason behind the worker's decision to be absent from work. If em-ployees have some other reason for not going to work on a particular day, it will be easier for them to decide not to go when they also feel that they are not really needed on the job. In short, it is most often a contributing and reinforc-ing cause of absenteeism. In some cases, however, the feeling of not being needed may be sufficient to prompt the employee to pursue other activities wherein the employee believes he or she is needed—even during scheduled work time. Hence, an employee's feeling of not being needed may function as a direct cause of absenteeism as well as a factor that contributes to and reinforces the decision to be absent where the primary motivation for the absence is something else. This theory incorporates elements of Maslow's hierarchy of needs theory.[7]

Strategic Withdrawal Theories

Workload Tolerance Theory

According to this theory, every individual has a specific amount of total work that can be tolerated. This workload varies substantially among individual workers and is composed of the total time involved in getting the job done—regular work hours, overtime hours, and travel hours to and from work. Time spent in one category reduces time available for another category. Thus, the more hours per day or week that a worker spends commuting to and from work, the fewer hours he or she will have available for straight time or overtime work. Whenever the maximum tolerance work level is reached, absenteeism occurs; the worker cannot tolerate any additional work, whatever its form. This theory borrows from several theories and is essentially a fatigue theory. Specifically, it borrows from both the Maslow (physiological need-rest) and Herzberg theories (hours of work as a hygiene factor).[8]

Coping Behavior Theory

Absenteeism can be regarded as "coping" behavior in the sense that the individual may deal with a given situation by being absent from work. If the job is viewed as especially stressful or boring or is regarded as lacking in meaning, one way of coping with this situation is to work hard, get ahead, and get promoted to a better job. Another way to cope with this situation is by not going to work. This theory contains features of Alderfer's "existence, relatedness, growth (ERG)" theory. Coping behavior is quite similar to Alderfer's concept of growth.[9]

In summary, psychological theories view the problem of absenteeism as a problem of individual motivation to attend work on a regular basis. Individual motivation focuses on three aspects of behavior: the direction of behavior, or choice among alternative courses of action (to attend or not to attend in the case of absenteeism); the strength of response or the effort expended once a choice is made (the effort that the employee expends to get to work); and the persistence of behavior, or how long the individual will continue trying to achieve the chosen objective (getting to work). The theories point out a number of variables that influence each of the above-noted aspects of behavior and, therefore, employee job attendance. Although incomplete, each adds to the understanding of absenteeism.

SOCIOLOGICAL THEORY

The major thrust of the various areas of sociology is toward the goal of understanding interdependent social behavior. The study encompasses society, its institutions, organizations, groups, and norms and rules. The last three are the most important for the study of absenteeism. Sociological theories of absenteeism focus on the impact that the interdependent variables within society, the organization, and the group have upon an individual's attendance behavior. Sociological theory thus seeks to explain attendance behavior in terms of forces within society and the group that facilitate or limit an individual's opportunity, capacity, and willingness to attend work. Important variables include social customs, infrastructure (that is, modes of transportation, communication, and so forth) and group mores. A few examples of sociological absenteeism theories should clarify their basic nature, focus, and thrust.

Conforming Behavior

Absenteeism may be regarded by some members of a work group as the accepted thing to do. It is valued by members of the group, and the individual who regularly attends work may be viewed as some kind of "brown nose" or management lackey. This theory assumes that employees have a need to be accepted as part of the group by their immediate peers and will succumb to social pressures from the group to be absent to gain that acceptance if absenteeism has become accepted group behavior. In addition, group pressures toward absenteeism are reinforced to the extent that the worker's family has condoned and sanctioned absenteeism as acceptable behavior. Conforming behavior theory is based on an extensive body of research on group behavior and its impact on individual behavior.[10]

Competition for Time

There are several kinds of activities that compete for the employee's work time. From a management point of view, the most legitimate competitive use of work time is its use for transaction of personal business that cannot occur except during business hours that coincide with the employee's working hours. This would include such things as going to the bank, seeing a lawyer or a doctor, conferring with a child's teacher or principal, and taking the car in for repairs. There are many such activities that may require employee absenteeism unless they can be attended to on the employee's own time.

Another alternative use of work time for some employees is a secondary income-producing activity. This could be a small business of some kind, a small farm, or a part-time job. On any given day, an employee might decide that it is more desirable, perhaps even more remunerative, to take time from a regular job and spend it on a secondary activity. This is particularly true for seasonal activities such as farming, operating a boat rental business, or plowing driveways and parking lots in the winter. Absenteeism is even more likely to occur when the secondary activity is one that the employee hopes to develop into the primary source of income either in the short run or after retirement.

Work time may also be used for various recreational activities. Indeed, a separate theory, "standard of living maximization," has evolved to trace the impact of leisure time upon employee work attendance. Proponents of this theory contend that workers view their standards of living in broader terms than simply income and the goods and services it will buy; one such broader term is leisure time. Accordingly, employees are pictured as striving to achieve an optimum balance between work and leisure in order to maximize their standard of living—absenteeism results when an employee finds scheduled hours of work reducing the hours of leisure necessary to enjoy the goods and services that work-generated income will buy. "Standard of living maximization" is discussed at this point for the light it sheds on an employee's possible alternative use of work time rather than as a separate theory of absenteeism.

Research on flexible hours of work (that is, "flexitime") tends to support the conclusions of "competition for time" theory. Studies of shiftwork and worker attendance, for example, indicate that the high incidence of absenteeism characteristic of weekends and days immediately preceding and following scheduled work cycles[11] can be reduced through use of flexitime.[12] Flexible working hours permit the worker to dovetail work with alternative uses of time in such a fashion that he or she can simultaneously engage in a number of activities without loss of work time, thus avoiding absenteeism. Although there are probably many other variables involved, competition for time appears to be an important cause of employee absences.

New Work Ethic

Many of today's labor force participants are imbued with the "Protestant work ethic." For them, work has value in and of itself; work is good per se. When hired by an employer, they believe they have entered a contract that mandates both regular and prompt work attendance. Regular and prompt work attendance is the "proper" way for workers to earn what they need and want of material goods, to get ahead, to improve themselves, and to achieve status in the community. Thus, work, in and of itself, is viewed as socially and morally desirable for both physical and spiritual well-being.

As important as the Protestant work ethic remains, there are those who point to its steady erosion as the major factor responsible for the rise in employee absenteeism.[13] Those who subscribe to this "new work ethic" theory contend that the Protestant work ethic no longer plays an important role in shaping the value systems of a growing number of labor force participants. Valuing work only for the income it generates and the economic security it provides rather than as a good in itself, the new generation worker has an increased propensity to be absent as dictated by the satisfaction of other needs. Attendance moves in tandem with the need for income, increasing when the need for income increases (for example, to purchase a major item) and decreasing when the need for income decreases (for example, after the item has been purchased and paid for). At the extreme are those individuals who would never attend (that is, hold a regular job) but for their inability to find an alternative nonworking method of satisfying basic physiological needs.

JURISPRUDENTIAL THEORY

Organizational policies and procedures affecting employee job attendance are the focus of this category. Many firms unwittingly create or compound their own attendance problems through ill-conceived, structured, or administered personnel policies—whether determined unilaterally or through collective bargaining. For example, some contract provisions governing the payment of wage and nonwage employee benefits provide direct incentives for employees to absent themselves from work. On the other hand, nonenforcement of absenteeism-related discipline makes absenteeism "easier"; it removes the penalty for irregular attendance. In both cases, the result is the same: a higher rate of absenteeism.

Employees judge and evaluate a firm's attitude toward absenteeism from the rules and regulations that it promulgates and administers; employee attitudes mirror those of management as expressed or implied through shop rules and their administration. A management attitude toward absenteeism that is perceived as cavalier due, for example, to lax enforcement of attendance-related discipline rules begets a similar attitude on the part of employees. Unfortunately, employees oftentimes misinterpret management actions that are intended merely to offset or minimize the impact of absenteeism. The simple act of creating and maintaining a list of qualified replacements for absentees may create the erroneous impression that absenteeism is normal and therefore acceptable; that management does not really care and therefore it does not really matter whether the employee comes to work on a regular basis. The requirement for advance notice of absences may give rise to similar misconceptions.

Paid days away from the job (for example, vacations, holidays, authorized leaves of absence, sick leave, bereavement time, and so on) provided either by labor agreement or personnel policy may also convey the impression that there is nothing wrong with occasional absences: "since they're willing to pay me for some kinds of absence days, and since my unscheduled absence doesn't cost them anything, they can't seriously object if I take an unpaid day off once in a while." While not a primary cause of absenteeism, these kinds of attitudes contribute to the problem, making it easier for the workers to decide not to attend when they have some other reason not to. Ironically then, many personnel policies and programs designed to reduce absenteeism or mitigate its effects inadvertently contribute to the problem. To avoid this embarrassing turn of events, management would be well advised to remind their employees constantly that absenteeism is a problem, that it does cost the company money, and that it will not be tolerated. Otherwise, employees may conclude that absenteeism is an accepted part of the labor relations landscape.[14]

DISABILITY THEORY

Theories within this classification explain absenteeism in terms of sickness or injuries that physically or mentally incapacitate the worker. Alcoholism, drug addiction, and self-inflicted disabilities fall within this category. The extent to which management "accepts" disability as an excuse for being absent depends on the nature and extent of disability. For example, management has shown a greater willingness to accept job-related, externally imposed disability (for example, a police officer being wounded in the line of duty) than non–job-related, self-inflicted disability (for example, incapacitation due to off-duty drug use). Employers have instituted a wide variety of different programs to reduce the causes of illness- and injury-related absences. These have included health education, awareness, and maintenance programs (for example, physical fitness programs); preventive medicine (for example, company-sponsored blood pressure checks and flu shots); chemical-dependence rehabilitation programs; comprehensive employee counseling, in-house in more routine cases and outside referral to private and community organizations for specialized cases; and safety programs, both on and off the job. Employers have also put into place health, accident, and disability insurance plans that are designed to soften the impact of disability.

There is very little theory involved with the notion that disability causes absenteeism; it is a simple statement of fact. What theory there is in "disability theory" primarily focuses upon explanations of why employees attribute so much of their absenteeism to disability. One hypothesis often advanced in this regard is the existence of a "welfare mentality": that health, accident, and disability insurance plans provide a vehicle for some employees, primarily the chronic absentee, to "purchase" time off at little out-of-pocket expenditure and little sacrifice of income. Time off can thus be purchased at bargain prices by those predisposed toward leisure—toward absence. Another explanation put forward is the emergence and rapid proliferation of so-called medical excuse mills in response to personnel policies that require doctors' statements to "excuse" absences attributed to sickness or disability. According to this explanation, there are some doctors who, for a small fee, will write an excuse for an employee's absence without examination or treatment but simply on the employee's word that he or she was ill or incapacitated. The ready availability of these excuses, or so the argument goes, has led employees to seek excused status for absences unrelated to disability or to extend absences that may have originally had a medical basis. Finally, and as noted earlier, there is the danger that the mere existence of medical records, excuses, and insurance will be misconstrued by employees as managerial acceptance and condonation of employee absences, thereby promoting a higher rate of absenteeism than would otherwise be the case.

SUMMARY

Theories of absenteeism abound. If nothing else, this fact reflects the importance society attaches to the control and resolution of the absenteeism problem. The body of knowledge concerning absenteeism, although extensive, is a hodgepodge of disjointed, incomplete, overlapping, and sometimes conflicting premises, hypotheses, and theories. Part of the problem can be traced to the

Figure 3.2.
An Integrated Model of Absenteeism Control

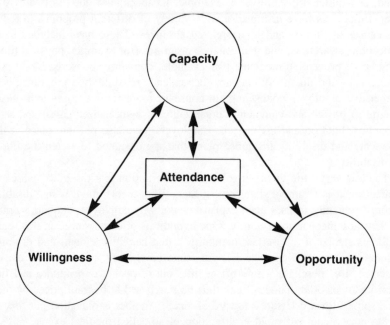

Capacity: The physiological and cognitive capabilities that enable an individual to attend work as scheduled.

Willingness: The psychological and emotional characteristics that influence the degree to which an individual is inclined to attend work as scheduled.

Opportunity: The particular configuration of situational factors surrounding an individual that enables or constrains work attendance and that are beyond the person's direct control.

Source: Adapted from Melvin Blumberg and Charles D. Pringle, "The Missing Opportunity in Organizational Research: Some Implications for a Theory of Work Performance," *Academy of Management Review* (October 1982) 7:565.

interdisciplinary nature of the inquiries. Grouping various theories of absenteeism into five broad categories helps clarify the assumptions upon which the theories contained therein are based and identify appropriate remedies for absenteeism caused thereby. While helping shed light upon the causes as well as possible remedies for absenteeism, this five-category (economic, psychological, sociological, jurisprudential, and disability) classification scheme does not bring the mass of theory into perfect perspective primarily because competing theories are not independent nor can they readily accommodate concepts unique yet critical to each. Simply put, there is a good deal of overlap between the five groups that cannot be eliminated because of incompatibility of terms, concepts, assumptions, and so on. Theories classified as economic, for example, are partly psychological, while some theories classified as psychological assume rational decision making—a characteristic of economic theories. For these reasons, the five-category classification scheme cannot be viewed as an integrated model of absenteeism.

Figure 3.2 suggests one method of combining various theories of absenteeism to produce an integrated, practical, policy-oriented model of absenteeism control. As illustrated, absenteeism theories are broadly classified as influencing an individual's capacity, willingness, or opportunity to work. This classification reduces overlap. More importantly, it is an eminently more useful description of worker behavior and, as such, absolutely critical to controlling and mitigating the deleterious impact of absenteeism upon the organization.

The following chapters will pursue the more useful theories discussed in the present chapter and also develop an integrated, policy-oriented model of absenteeism control along the lines of the model pictured in Figure 3.2. The reader must keep in mind, however, that individual worker and organizational characteristics will condition or qualify the success obtained through specific policy prescriptions. Policy pitfalls and policy alternatives, therefore, will also be noted when and where appropriate.

NOTES

1. Richard Boynton et al., *Absenteeism and General Motors: A Step toward Understanding* (Detroit: General Motors Personnel Administration and Development Staff, January 1975), pp. 5–14.

2. Stacy Adams, "Inequity in Social Exchange," in L. Berkowitz (ed.) *Advances in Experimental Social Psychology* (New York: Academic Press, 1965).

3. Victor H. Vroom, *Work and Motivation* (New York: John Wiley & Sons, 1964).

4. Leon Festinger, *A Theory of Cognitive Dissonance* (Stanford, Calif.: Stanford University Press, 1957).

5. Vroom, *Work and Motivation*, pp. 14–15.

6. J. Richard Hackman and G. R. Oldham, "Motivation through the Design of Work: Test of a Theory," *Organizational Behavior and Human Performance* (August 1976), 16:250–279.

7. A. H. Maslow, "A Theory of Human Motivation," *Psychological Review* (July 1943), 40:370–396.

8. Frederick Hersberg et al., *The Motivation to Work*, 2d ed. (New York: John Wiley & Sons, 1959), p. 141.

9. Clayton P. Alderfer, *Existence, Relatedness, and Growth: Human Needs in Organizational Settings* (New York: Free Press, 1972).

10. Leonard Berkowitz, "Group Standards, Cohesiveness, and Productivity," *Human Relations* (1954), 7 (4):509–519.

11. Nigel Nicholson and Paul Jackson, "Shiftwork and Absence: An Analysis of Temporal Trends," *Journal of Occupational Psychology* (1978), 54 (4):127–137.

12. R. T. Golembiewski and C. W. Proehl, Jr., "A Survey of the Empirical Literature of Flexible Working Hours: Character and Consequences of a Major Innovation," *Academy of Management Review* (October 1978), 3:837–853.

13. Reinhard Bendix and Max Weber, *An Intellectual Portrait* (Garden City, N.Y.: Doubleday, 1960), p. 266.

14. Clarence R. Deitsch and David A. Dilts, "Getting Absent Workers Back on the Job: The Case of General Motors," *Business Horizons* (September/October 1981), 24:52–58.

4 Toward a General Theory of Absenteeism

> When a man has not a good reason for doing a thing, he has one good reason for letting it alone.
>
> Rev. Thomas Scott
> *Commentary on the Bible*

Reverend Scott identified one of the three general causes of absenteeism: lack of motivation to attend work. The truth in this quote from Reverend Scott is undisputable, yet this axiom alone does not constitute a general theory of absenteeism, since several other causes of absenteeism are known to exist. Often, a firm or government agency will experience absenteeism resulting from several different causes. The management of an organization that is successful in identifying one cause of absenteeism and applying appropriate policy measures will find that the applicable measures of absenteeism are little affected due to several other causes being present in the work environment—much the same as the proverbial Dutch boy with his finger in the dike.

Policy prescriptions for absenteeism must be based on a generalized, easily understood, and operable theory of absenteeism. The word *theory* should not be construed as taking the present discussion from real world environs and heading into the caverns of academic discourse. A good theory is one that describes the real world. There are several things known about why people act the way they do in the work environment; admittedly, there are several unanswered questions but enough is known to build a good model of absenteeism and use it as a basis of effective personnel policy.

This chapter focuses on what is presently known of the economic, sociological, and psychological influences on employee attendance behavior. The purpose of this review of literature is to lay the foundation for the integrative absentee control program presented in the following chapters. A word of warning is necessary at this point. There is a substantial body of literature concerning absenteeism but the preponderance of empirical studies has focused on narrow aspects of the problem and many of the descriptive (nonempirical studies) are based more on ideology than on logical constructs.[1]

A BASIC MODEL

Employee work attendance can be thought of as being dependent upon three conditions that are necessary and sufficient to ensure employee attendance.[2] This simply means that each of the conditions must be fulfilled and if they are employees will report for work. If any one of the three conditions is not satisfied, then employees will not report for work. These three conditions are: employees are able to attend (*ABILITY*); employees are willing to report to work (*MOTI-VATION*); and employees are given a chance to report for work (*OPPORTU-NITY*). If able, willing, and given the opportunity, employees will attend, but if willing and able and a snow storm prevents them, employees will not attend.

Figure 4.1 presents a diagrammatical illustration of the basic model of absenteeism discussed in this chapter. The circles contain the three necessary and sufficient conditions for employee attendance, with the various influences on these conditions contained in the surrounding rectangles. It should be obvious from the flows indicated in Figure 4.1 that ability, opportunity, and willingness to attend are not independent of one another and each condition is influenced by numerous factors.

Even though Figure 4.1 presents a rather complex picture of employee absenteeism behavior, it is a useful frame of reference and is reasonably descriptive of reality. The discussion that follows is based on the model presented in Figure 4.1 and the reader will wish to refer back to the model periodically to avoid narrowly focusing on one set of concepts rather than the "big picture."

WILLINGNESS TO ATTEND

Employee motivation to report for work is a decisional variable that is controlled by the individual employee. Employers can only influence how the employees make the decisions to attend or be absent. Economic, sociological, and psychological variables all come into play in the employees' decision-making processes. It is often assumed by employers that employees will be motivated by the ability to earn a wage. If this assumption is correct and if employees are not attending work then all an employer must do is to pay an attractive wage and threaten to discharge employees who fail to report for work. This is a simple and an appealing approach to absenteeism control but it is fraught with dangerous omissions. In an economic sense, what may be an attractive wage in the employer's view may not be so attractive to employees. Economists cite two reasons for this observation. Employees value both leisure and income; if a sufficient income is obtained but little or no leisure is available to enjoy the income then employees will offer fewer hours for work. High wages may result

Figure 4.1.
A Model of Employee Absenteeism

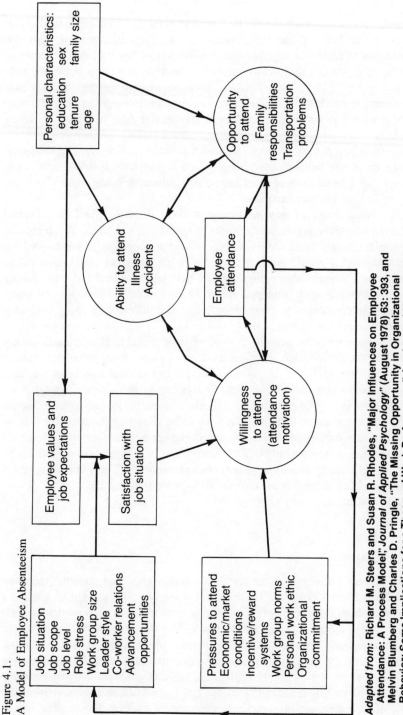

Adapted from: Richard M. Steers and Susan R. Rhodes, "Major Influences on Employee Attendance: A Process Model", *Journal of Applied Psychology*" (August 1978) 63: 393, and Melvin Blumberg and Charles D. Pringle, "The Missing Opportunity in Organizational Behavior: Some Implications for a Theory of Work Performance," *Academy of Management Review* (October 1982) 7: 560-569.

in employees cutting back the hours offered to employers. Further complicating matters is the fact that the attractiveness of any wage is dependent upon the alternatives available to an employee. Public school teachers often remain in teaching even though they could utilize their training and skills in other activities that pay a higher monetary wage. Teachers often cite, as their main reason for staying in teaching, nonmonetary rewards such as contributing to the students' academic progress or the enjoyment they receive from working with young people.

Industrial psychology is less concerned with what specific types of things influence employee behavior. Industrial psychologists have focused their attention on two general categories of behavioral influences in the work place: job content and job context variables.[3]

Job content variables may be defined as those behavioral factors embodied in the requirements, rights, and rewards of specific employment. A job content problem frequently associated with blue collar employment is job safety. All other things being equal, the more hazardous a job, the more absenteeism would be expected. Witness the higher rates of absenteeism associated with mining and manufacturing when compared with those for finance and banking—job safety undoubtedly contributes to these absenteeism rate differentials along with several other important factors.

Job context variables may be defined as those behavioral influences associated with the environment in which work takes place. Such behavioral factors as physical surroundings, role stress, work group size, and co-worker relations are job context variables. Job context is also known to influence employee attendance behavior. For example, in the case of supervisory personnel, a hostile union will often cause first line managers to be absent at greater rates than in work environments characterized by union-management cooperation.

In practice, it is often difficult to identify and isolate job content influences from those properly identified as job context variables. These distinctions are drawn solely as a conceptual tool to aid in understanding the sources of employee motivation.

Job Content

Job content encompasses the responsibilities, rights, and rewards (the three Rs) of a particular position. These three Rs are typically defined in a job description which delineates, often in only general terms, what a particular position is within a firm or government agency. The various aspects of job content are not artificially constructed but are dictated by the goals, needs, and environment in which the employer's organization must function. Job content, job analysis, and job design are themselves the subjects of several lengthy texts and cannot be given full treatment here, but a few specifics must be discussed because of their strategic importance to absenteeism control. The present discussion, for the sake of brevity, will focus on the three Rs to the extent that they directly affect employee motivation to attend work.

The responsibilities of a particular job are what employees are paid for performing for the employer. Responsibilities will differ substantially across occupations, levels within an organization, and industries. Work has different meanings to different people for different reasons. For example, a research scientist may live for his work, while an assembly-line worker lives as a result of his work. The motivational techniques to be applied to each of these two workers must account for the way in which each worker sees his responsibilities.

As a practical illustration, assume that both the research scientist and the assembly-line worker are dissatisfied with their jobs. It might be appropriate to rotate the assembly-line worker to other jobs that require the performance of different functions and the use of different skills. If the worker was placing bearings on an axle at the rate of 25 sets per minute, it might prove productive to assign him to an inventory department. In so doing, the routine is broken and boredom may give way to real interest in mastering a challenging new job. If boredom was the employee's problem, then the motivation to attend work can be rekindled. On the other hand, if the research scientist becomes bored with a project in chemistry it would make little sense to assign the chemist to a shipping department; a change in specific lines of scientific inquiry within the employee's area of expertise is much more logical.

Herein lies the problem with the current fad of job enrichment. Job enrichment can be a useful technique to enhance productivity and to motivate employees to attend work. A cardinal rule with any change in job content is that employees and specific duties must be matched.[4] This is not to say that employees cannot be placed in positions requiring unfamiliar duties, but those duties must be within the employee's capabilities and not create underemployment of workers. This sounds like a complicated process requiring extensive testing, record keeping, and job analysis and design. In fact, the more technical or skilled a position, the more an employer will have to invest in testing, record keeping, and job analysis and design. For the bulk of unskilled positions, little except common sense and good managerial judgment is required to make job enrichment an effective tool for motivating employees to attend work.[5]

Responsibilities and duties of a specific job are also directly related to job satisfaction, hence to employee values and job stress.[6] Job satisfaction, in turn, influences employee willingness to attend work. If the duties of a specific job are challenging and intrinsically rewarding to the incumbent, then that employee will be satisfied with the job, all other things being equal. Problems arise when the required duties result in employee dissatisfaction. If, for example, the employee is incapable of performing the required duties (overemployment) or the employee becomes bored with an assignment that does not use his or her potential (underemployment), then the employee becomes dissatisfied. This dissatisfaction is typically manifested in the expression of complaints, formal grievances, and withdrawal from the organization. Withdrawal can be accomplished through several routes, such as isolating one's self from co-workers, avoiding certain tasks, quitting one's job, or through absenteeism. How specific individuals will respond to job dissatisfaction of this nature is virtually impossible to forecast. Further complicating matters is the fact that job satisfaction is often cited as the transmission mechanism between under or overemployment and absenteeism.[7]

Responsibilities of any job affect the attendance behavior of employees as illustrated in the immediately preceding paragraphs through various mechanisms. Rewards and rights will also substantially affect employees' motivation to attend. The monetary rewards and rights granted employees for service rendered to the employer form what is properly called compensation. Recognition through advancement opportunities, higher wages or salaries, increased benefits, and more rights (for example, job security) for a job well done will motivate employees to participate in the employer's operations (that is, attend work). On the other hand, a failure to recognize a job well done by an appropriate distribution of rewards and rights will result in disincentives for continued employee participation and will result in absenteeism—especially among the more capable workers whose aspirations have been left unsatisfied. It must be remembered that compensation must be tied directly to the performance of duties or the motivation to attend work will be lost.

Monetary rewards, as previously discussed, are important determinants of employee attendance behavior.[8] There are several factors closely related to monetary compensation that are of critical importance in understanding employee motivation to attend work. Whether or not an employee's income from work is the sole support for the household is generally recognized as an important determinant of the employee's motivation to attend.[9] If other sources of household support are readily available then it is less critical for the household survival or maintenance of a desired standard of living that the employee regularly attend work. If the employee's income from employment is the sole support for the household then it becomes more critical for the employee to be regular in attendance.

Aspirations of employees are also important in understanding employee attendance behavior. One study has shown that education may influence employee attendance behavior through aspirations.[10] More educated workers typically have higher levels of aspiration (for example, higher expectations of advancement, challenging work, rewards, and rights). If such employees are given the opportunity (assuming their ability) to advance and earn more rewards (on their own merits), their attendance rates will be higher. This makes sense from two perspectives, that employees will be more satisfied with their jobs and they will be more committed to quality performance—hence regular attendance. On the other hand, highly educated workers in less demanding positions or those who perceive themselves as having limited advancement opportunities tend to be absent at a greater rate or simply quit to seek employment elsewhere.

Effective performance appraisal is an absolute must if white collar absentee-ism is to be reduced. This is not to say that performance appraisal is unimpor-tant in blue collar occupations. The performance of all employees must be pe-riodically examined to determine who should be promoted, given increases in rewards and rights, and who should not. High performers who are rewarded or advanced at the same rate as low performers will quickly become dissatisfied because of inequities in promotions and rewards. This may be of greater sig-nificance in white collar occupations due to the more technical and professional requirements of these occupations. Blue collar skilled workers such as tool and dye makers face essentially the same dangers as white collar employees. The basic rule here is simple. Equity demands that performance, good or bad, be recognized and appropriately dealt with. Inequity will breed absenteeism and higher turnover rates.

Demographics seem to affect employee attendance behavior. This is, in part, due to the compensation system and method utilized to assign employee rights. Older employees appear to be absent less frequently and are lost for less time than younger employees. In firms and agencies where seniority is either the sole or central determinant of salaries (for example, public school teacher salary schedules) and job security (for example, union contracts) then older employ-ees, by virtue of greater seniority, are compensated at higher rates and have greater rights.[11] Job satisfaction, fulfillment of aspirations, and greater com-mitment to the employer are likely responses that, in turn, should serve to re-duce the absenteeism rates of older employees. Alternative explanations of the observed lower absenteeism rates for older employees do exist. The most ap-pealing of these alternative explanations are the life cycle hypothesis and work ethic. Some scholars contend that older employees have fewer alternative uses of their time and therefore are most likely to be regular in their attendance. Some managers and academics seem to hold to the position that the generation of workers who grew up during the depression have a stronger work ethic and this contributes to their more regular attendance. There is little credible evi-dence to date to support either of these alternative explanations for lower ab-senteeism rates among older workers.

Whether these demographic factors are actually job content or job context influences is subject to debate. Since these influences are compensation related and job specific the authors have chosen to discuss these variables in the job content section of this chapter, but equally persuasive arguments can be made that these influences are outside the scope of a specific job and are therefore job context variables. The truth of the matter is left to the reader to decide.

Job Context

Job context influences can affect employee attendance behavior much the same as job content factors. Job context refers to the various elements that make up the work environment. Such factors as co-worker relations, work group size, physical environment, and managerial leadership styles can all influence an employee's motivation to attend work.

Co-worker relations have an obvious influence on the overall satisfaction of a worker with a specific job. It has been pointed out elsewhere in this text that if co-workers are frequently absent from work then replacements must be transferred to unfamiliar jobs. This shifting of employees often is a substantial source of work force unrest, especially if chronically absent workers are assigned to distasteful jobs.[12]

Several other factors in co-worker relations are of sufficient importance to warrant brief discussion. Discipline must be handled in an evenhanded manner. For offenses warranting discipline, workers expect that management will issue penalties for misbehavior, especially in cases where the offender threatens a co-worker or endangers a co-worker. If the work force cannot rely on management to maintain a safe and orderly workplace then workers may seek to avoid unsafe or disorderly environments by quitting or being absent.

Disruptive employees are of concern in at least two contexts that are not directly related to the firm's disciplinary policies. Professional and technical employees who must focus their attention on complicated tasks, engage in research, or deal with the public are often distraught by interruptions, horseplay, or other such distractions. The distractions retard professional growth and earnings potential and create stress. Management must seek to minimize the unnecessary distractions in a work environment if employee withdrawal is to be avoided. Employees on piece rate compensation systems are often very competitive. Occasionally, this competitiveness results in employees disrupting fellow employees, especially if productive employees endanger current rate structures. If piece rates are used for compensating employees then management must make a concerted effort to ensure that competition among employees does not focus on rate busting and become dysfunctional. This requires fair rates being set and a substantial amount of managerial control being exercised over breaks, lunch periods, and down time.

Work group size refers to the number of persons in the employee's work group (that is, crew, department, office, and so on). Larger work groups generally experience higher absenteeism rates than do smaller groups.[13] The reasons for this observation are somewhat complicated. It appears that managerial control is more difficult with extremely large work groups but there are other contributing factors. Larger work groups have greater difficulties with intragroup communications and there is a greater likelihood of group members having different goals, backgrounds, and personal expectations resulting in greater friction within the group and more employee withdrawal.

The physical environment of the work place is also of great importance, as noted elsewhere in this volume. Clean, pleasant, and safe surroundings make the workplace more appealing and workers are more likely to be satisfied with such an environment. Often, the nature of specific types of employment constrain what may be done with this job and management must make every effort to ensure the most pleasant and safe work environment possible.

The quality of work life movement has focused considerable attention on the physical environment of work. Upgrading of the physical environment is an important and tangible portion of any quality of work life program, but managers must be careful to consider the remaining portions of the work environment and not focus solely on physical surroundings. To date, many of the failed quality of work life programs seem to have focused too much attention on the tangible, ignoring other job context factors.

Leadership style is the manner in which managerial employees attempt to influence subordinates. There is a substantial literature concerning the effects of leadership style on organizational effectiveness and absenteeism.[14] Leadership style depends substantially on the situation in which leadership must occur. For example, an authoritarian style necessary to accomplishing military missions probably would not be effective in manufacturing and would be an absolute disaster in an academic department. In general, leadership styles have a more direct impact on organizational effectiveness than on absenteeism. Ineffective organizations will typically create disharmony and employee job dissatisfaction which then results in increased absenteeism.

The discussion of job context presented here focuses on but a few of the factors known to influence the work environment, but these factors are the most critical in the determination of absenteeism rates. Employees who choose to absent themselves from work often do so because something is amiss in their work environment and job context must be accounted for if any absenteeism control policy is to be effective.

ABILITY TO ATTEND

Earlier in this chapter it was pointed out that one of the assumptions traditionally made concerning absenteeism was that employees were free to attend work or be absent as they wished. There was no involuntary absenteeism. This assumption can lead to absence measurement errors and a considerable amount of confusion in formulating appropriate absenteeism control policies. It is essential that voluntary and involuntary absenteeism be clearly distinguished. There are many situations where an employee may be willing to attend but unable to do so. Illnesses and accidents are the most common causes of inability to attend work and are the focal points of the discussion presented here.

Poor health is a primary cause of absenteeism. Personal characteristics are significant factors in health-related absenteeism. Unfortunately, it is quite difficult to obtain valid statistics on absences due to illness. There are a number of reasons for this problem: medical analysis is judgmental and at least partly based on the patient's statements; follow-up can be time consuming and expensive; employees may resent being checked up on; and problems of alcoholism and drug abuse, which are difficult to detect and may not be completely involuntary, are included in this category.

There are a number of indications that at least some absenteeism due to illness is not legitimate. For example, unpaid absenteeism is lower and is related to selected attitudinal and biographical variables, but paid absences are unpredictable.[15] It has also been claimed that "well pay" plans, ones that reward attendance, reduce absenteeism, although other studies question not only the claim, but label the approach bribery.[16] Finally, absence rates are related to organizational control policies and practices (rewards and sanctions) that relate to absenteeism.[17] It appears that employees who might normally be absent because of illness are not always ill enough to pass up organizational rewards or avoid organizational sanctions.

It is possible that absences due to illness could be too low. This would occur if an employee stayed on the job while ill. Most likely, productivity would decline, others would be exposed to illness, and, if jobs are interdependent, the productivity of other employees would be reduced. A similar set of problems could occur if an employee returned to work too soon after an illness. In either case, absenteeism would be too low. Although there are individual cases where an employee's absenteeism is too low, it is much more likely that employee absenteeism for alleged illness is too high.

Organizations engage in a number of practices to reduce illness and illness-related absenteeism. Many firms maintain medical facilities with trained nurses and doctors present. They provide instruction in health programs and provide facilities for exercise and training. They also equip the plant with equipment to control heat, light, noise, vapors, and other environmental hazards.

In summary, employees may be absent because they do not have the ability to get to work even though they may want to attend. One of the primary reasons for inability to attend is illness. Data on absences due to illness are unreliable because much illness is self-reported and -diagnosed. Although it is possible for reported figures for absenteeism due to illness to be low, it is more likely that these figures will exceed the true magnitude of illness-related absenteeism.

Accidents are another cause of absenteeism that falls into the category of inability to attend. Obviously, an injured worker may be unable to attend, but many injuries are difficult to detect, for example, some back injuries. As in the case of illness, the data on absenteeism due to accidents is probably invalid. There are several reasons for the lack of validity: the definition of accident (is it the event or the consequence of the event) is not precise; firms do not keep accurate records; self-reporting hides some accidents; experience rating for accident insurance premium determination encourages nonreporting; and frequently, illness and accident absences are combined.

Figure 4.1 indicates that personal variables are important moderators of ability to attend work through their impact on illness and accidents. There are a number of theories based on personal variables. Accident proneness theory suggests that some people have innate tendencies to engage in unsafe behavior. For example, it is maintained that a small percentage of the workers have a large percentage of the accidents. However, when other factors are removed there is only weak support for this argument.[18] There is some support for the theory that a person's ability to cope with stress influences the person's risk of being involved in an accident. Stress, in turn, has been found to be directly related to absenteeism. Ability to cope with stress varies with individuals. Goals-freedom-alertness theory maintains that people who work in environments that permit and reward an employee's own goal setting encourage alertness and that these employees have fewer accidents. Research suggests that some people respond to such environments while others do not, thus personal characteristics are again the main determinants.[19] Perhaps the best support for personal variables theories (age, and so on) of accidents is Bureau of Labor Statistics data on the accident-age relationship.[20] Younger workers have more accidents.

Absenteeism due to the consequences of accidents could be too low. Injured workers might hide injuries to avoid lost time. They might also return to work before recovery is complete. Although there are probably more cases of absenteeism for noninjuries, rates that are either too low or too high are costly to organizations.

Organizations engage in a number of practices to reduce absenteeism because of injury. Most of these efforts focus on accident prevention. Included are employee job training, equipment and workplace design, and various incentives for injury-free performance. The effectiveness of these accident prevention programs is difficult to assess as data are not available. Frequently, a number of changes are made simultaneously and it is difficult to determine which change is responsible for reducing accidents.

OPPORTUNITY TO ATTEND

An employee may be willing to work and be able to work but not have the opportunity to attend work. Frequently, variables that deny the opportunity to attend are considered under ability to attend, but they are different enough to merit separate analysis. This category includes two important groups of variables: family responsibilities and transportation problems.

Personal characteristics of the individual play a significant role in the relationship between family responsibilities and absenteeism (sex, age, and family size). Higher absenteeism rates among women and the positive relationships between absenteeism and the number of dependents are statistics that support the family responsibility argument. Also, some women drop out of the labor force during the child-raising years.

However, support for the statistics is questioned by findings that the age and marital status of women were not related to absenteeism.[21] It is likely that as more and more married women enter or remain in the labor force, family responsibilities will become much more a joint man-woman responsibility. There is some evidence that absenteeism can be reduced if employees are given time to conduct personal and family activities. For example, the four-day work week and flexible work schedules have been found to reduce absenteeism in some situations.[22]

Organizations and even government agencies are beginning to recognize and provide for employee problems related to family responsibilities. In addition to flexible work hours, they are providing day care centers for the children of employees. Efforts are made to adjust work schedules of two-earner families and some families and some companies even permit job sharing (two or more persons sharing a full-time job).

Research and experience lead to conflicting conclusions regarding the influence of difficulties of getting to work on absenteeism. Travel distance, travel time, and weather conditions have been found to influence employee attendance.[23] In an analysis of work-related problems 33 percent of the respondents regarded transportation problems as "sizable" or "great." It is probable that this problem would be even more severe for low income workers.

Organizations have traditionally assumed that transportation was the employee's personal problem. The firm usually made no arrangements or provided only for a few top managers and outside salespersons. Recent concern for energy conservation led some firms and government agencies to investigate employer- or agency-operated buses and employer-sponsored car-pooling programs. Transportation facilities appear to have evolved from a prerequisite to at least a recognized need. Of course, the availability of adequate transportation facilities is an important consideration in plant site selection.

THE MODEL AS A SYSTEM

In Figure 4.1, the model indicates separate classifications of variables joined by arrows to indicate relationships. The model should be considered a process. Each variable influences and is influenced by others. For example, family responsibilities are influenced by personal variables that provide both obstacles to and incentives for work attendance. Leadership style may be a significant factor in employee willingness to attend. In turn, employee attendance records may elicit given leadership styles. Thus, the model is a dynamic one in which employee absence or attendance leads to changes in the job situation that in turn influence subsequent attendance behavior.

SUMMARY

Research on employee absenteeism indicates that it is influenced by a great number of variables. These complex and changing variables may be classified as personal, job situational, and environmental. They exert their influence on employee attendance through influence on the willingness, ability, and opportunity to attend. Some of the variables are subject to employee or management control while others are beyond control. In essence, the nature of the job interacts with personal values and aspirations to produce a level of job satisfaction. The level of job satisfaction in conjunction with pressures to attend generate a willingness to attend or a motivation to attend. The relationship between the willingness to attend and actual attendance is not sufficient, however, as an employee must also have the ability and opportunity to attend. The feedback from actual attendance influences perceptions of the job situation and changes employee aspiration levels. These changes, in turn, alter the impact of variables that exert pressure to attend and motivation to attend. The model includes the cyclical nature of the variables and forces that influence employee absenteeism.

The relative importance of the various influences varies over time, place, and with personal characteristics of the employees. For example, participative leadership styles may be very desirable to some employees and be an important consideration in the job situation. Other employees may be almost completely unconcerned with leadership. It is also possible that employees may be able to substitute one desirable attribute for another. A highly supportive work group might compensate for the boredom of a routine repetitive work. It appears logical to assume that the more attributes of work that can be made attractive the higher the probability of attendance will be. The attributes may also be cumulative.

It should also be remembered that some of the variables act directly on work attendance, while others serve as moderator variables. Some may also serve to promote dissatisfaction if not available but exert little influence if available. Human behavior is not always predictable from values, attitudes, and beliefs. Sometimes, the same attitudes generate different behavior. Nonetheless, the model is based on the best research and experience available and is presented solely to demonstrate to the reader that any program for absence control must be tailored to the specific firm. We now turn our attention to absence control in the remaining chapters of this book.

NOTES

1. Richard M. Steers and Susan R. Rhodes, "Major Influences on Employee Attendance: A Process Model," *Journal of Applied Psychology* (August 1978), 63:391–407.

2. Melvin Blumberg and Charles D. Pringle, "The Missing Opportunity in Organizational Behavior: Some Implications for a Theory of Work Performance," *Academy of Management Review* (October 1982), 7:560–569.

3. Frederick Herzberg, Bernard Mausner, and Barbara Block Snyderman, *The Motivation to Work*, 2d ed. (New York: John Wiley & Sons, 1959).

4. J. Richard Hackman, "On the Coming Demise of Job Enlargement," in E. L. Cass and F. G. Zumimer (eds.), *Man and Work in Society* (New York: Van Nostrand, 1975), p. 98.

5. J. R. Hackman and Greg R. Oldman, "Motivation through the design of Work: Test of a Theory," *Organizational Behavior and Human Performance* (August 1976), 16:250–279.

6. Nina Gupta and Terry A. Beehr, "Job Stress and Employee Behaviors," *Organizational Behavior and Human Performance* (June 1979), 23:373–387.

7. G. P. Latham, L. L. Cummings, and T. R. Mitchell, "Behavioral Strategies to Improve Productivity," *Organizational Dynamics* (Winter 1981), 9:4–23.

8. See Steven G. Allen, "Compensation, Safety and Absenteeism: Evidence from the Paper Industry," *Industrial and Labor Relations Review* (January 1981), 34:207–218; and Donald Winkler, "The Effects of Sick-Leave Policy on Teacher Absenteeism," *Industrial and Labor Relations Review* (January 1980), 33:232–240.

9. Dale Fitzgibbons and Michael Moch, "Employee Absenteeism: A Multivariate Analysis with Replication," *Organizational Behavior and Human Performance* (December 1980), 26:349–372.

10. Daniel G. Spencer and Richard M. Steers, "The Influence of Personal Factors and Perceived Work Experiences on Employee Turnover and Absenteeism," *Academy of Management Journal* (September 1980), 23:567–572.

11. S. Kerr, "On the Folly of Rewarding A, While Hoping for B," *Academy of Management Journal* (December 1975), 18:769–783.

12. C. R. Deitsch and D. A. Dilts, "Getting Absent Workers Back on the Job: The Case of General Motors," *Business Horizons* (September/October 1981), 24:52–58.

13. Steven Markham, Fred Dansereau, Jr., and Joseph Alutto, "Group Size and Absenteeism Rates: A Longitudinal Analysis," *Academy of Management Journal* (December 1982), 25:921–927.

14. For example, see Ralph K. White and Ronald Lippitt, *Autocracy and Democracy: An Experimental Inquiry* (New York: Harper & Row, 1960); David Powers and Stanley Seashore, "Predicting Organizational Effectiveness with a Four Factor Theory of Leadership," *Administrative Science Quarterly* (September 1966), 11:238–263.

15. John F. Baum, "Effectiveness of an Attendance Control Policy in Reducing Chronic Absenteeism," *Personnel Psychololgy* (Spring 1978), 31:71–81.

16. Miriam Rothman, "Can Alternatives to Sick Pay Plans Reduce Absenteeism?" *Personnel Journal* (October 1981), 60:788–790.

17. Dan R. Dalton and James L. Perry, "Absenteeism and the Collective Bargaining Agreement: An Empirical Test," *Academy of Management Journal* (June 1981), 24(2):425–431.

18. Willard Kerr, "Contemporary Theories of Safety Psychology," *Journal of Social Psychology* (1957), 45(3):3–9.

19. Hans Selye, *The Stress of Life*, rev. ed. (New York: McGraw-Hill, 1976).

20. Norman Root, "Injuries among Workers Are Fewer among Older Employees," *Monthly Labor Review* (March 1981), 104:31.

21. Steven G. Allen, "An Empirical Model of Work Attendance," *The Review of Economics and Statistics* (February 1980), 63:77–78.

22. Graham L. Staines and Robert P. Quinn, "American Workers Evaluate the Quality of Their Jobs," *Monthly Labor Review* (January 1979), 102:3–12.

23. Allen, "An Empirical Model of Work Attendance," pp. 77–87.

5 An Integrated Approach to Absenteeism Control

> This thou must always bear in mind what is the nature of the whole, and what is my nature, and how this is related to that, and what kind of part it is of what kind of a whole; and that there is no one who hinder thee from always doing and saying the things which thou art a part.
>
> Marcus Aurelius
> *Meditations* 2.2

As is evident from the discussions presented in the previous chapters, absenteeism is a complex problem. The exact causes and nature of absenteeism may vary from one organization to another and from occupation to occupation. Yet there are several generalizations that seem to be supported throughout the majority of "real world" situations and by the preponderance of the academic literature. It is this narrow range of truth upon which this chapter is based.

The specific purpose of this chapter is to suggest an approach to absenteeism control (that is, a model of absenteeism control) based on an integration of appropriate economic incentives, disciplinary policies, and work environment. While this control program accounts for the major influences on employee attendance behavior, it must be remembered that the program must be tailored to the specific needs and circumstances in evidence in each organization. Blind adoption of any generalized policy recommendation is at best unwise. While various alternatives will be suggested and pitfalls pointed out, it is still up to the individual manager to exercise care in accepting or rejecting the suggestions presented here.

STRUCTURING THE INCENTIVE PROGRAM

Economists are known, especially by practitioners, for the endless array of assumptions upon which their analyses are based. One in particular, rationality, is common to virtually all economic theorizing; the model of employee work attendance (absenteeism) is no exception. As used here, it holds that employees, either white or blue collar, who absent themselves from work may do so because, from their vantage point, it is the rational response to the incentives built into the organization's compensation and personnel policies.[1] This section analyzes the incentive programs for both blue collar and white collar workers and suggests various ways that they might be restructured for maximum and effective absenteeism control.

Blue Collar Employees

Table 5.1 presents the relation between hours worked and the corresponding effective hourly wage rates inherent in one type of blue collar wage structure that is currently used by many firms. Table 5.1 assumes a marginal effective hourly wage rate (this is, nominal contractual wage rate) of $4 per hour and employee benefits valued at $150 per week, or $3.75 per hour based on a 40-hour workweek. Although the marginal effective hourly wage rate (column 5) remains constant at $4 per hour throughout the week until overtime rates go into effect, the average effective hourly wage rate (column 4) declines over the workweek until additional hours worked at extremely high overtime premiums again pull the average effective hourly wage rate up. This behavior results from the fixed component of compensation (that is, employee benefits valued at $150

Table 5.1.
Relationship between Hours Worked and Average Effective Hourly Wage Rates Where Employee Benefits Are Not Tied to Hours Worked

(1) Hours Worked	(2) Total Weekly Earnings[1]	(3) Earnings Per Eight Hours Worked	(4) Average Effective Hourly Wage Rate (col. 2 ÷ col. 1)	(5) Marginal Effective Hourly Wage Rate (Contractual Wage Rate) (Δ col. 2 ÷ Δ col. 1)[*]
0	$150[2]	—		$4
8	182	$32	$22.75	4
16	214	32	13.37	4
24	246	32	10.25	4
32	278	32	8.69	4
40	310	32	7.75[2]	4
48	358[3]	48	7.46	6
56	422[4]	64	7.54	8

1. These figures include the monetary equivalent of employee benefits—$150 per week.
2. Although employee benefits are assumed to cost the employer $150 per week per worker or $3.75 per hour pro-rated over a scheduled 40-hour week, the $3.75 per hour cost of employee benefits is realized only when the employee works the scheduled 40-hour week. The cost of employee benefits is much greater when the worker is absent from work. For example, if a worker is absent one day, the average hourly cost to the employer of that worker's fringe benefits is $4.69.
3. This figure is calculated based upon 40 hours at the straight-time nominal wage of $4 per hour, 8 hours at time-and-a-half ($6 per hour), and employee benefits of $150.
4. This figure is calculated based upon 40 hours at $4 per hour, 8 hours at time-and-a-half ($6 per hour), 8 hours at double time ($8 per hour), plus employee benefits of $150.
* Change in column 2 divided by change in column 1.

per week) that, for purposes of highlighting the major causes of absenteeism discussed in this chapter, are assumed to be paid regardless of the number of hours worked. Note that the degree to which the factors identified in this chapter promote absenteeism depends on the relationship between the value of employee benefits and the number of hours worked per week. Maximum impact occurs where these two variables are not related. Hence, for the purpose of the analysis, we assume that there is no relationship between the value of employee benefits and the number of hours worked.

Table 5.2 shows the impact of tying employee benefits directly to the number of hours worked by the employee. Under the tied wage structure, employee benefits are available only to the extent that work is performed (at the rate of $3.75 for each hour worked). For example, an employee working 16 hours would be entitled to $124 (see columns 1 and 2B), $60 of which would represent a payment in kind for employee benefits (16 × $3.75). To become entitled to the full value of employee benefits ($150 in Table 5.2), an employee would be required to work the scheduled 40-hour workweek ($3.75 × 40 = $150). As column 3B of Table 5.2 indicates, tying employee benefits to hours worked increases the marginal effective hourly wage rate from $4 per hour (see column 3A) to $7.75 per hour; the difference is the hourly employee benefit rate of $3.75. For a scheduled 40-hour workweek, the marginal effective hourly wage rate is the same under both the tied and untied wage structures. The employee benefit–tied wage structure of this table could easily be derived from the untied wage structure of Table 5.1 through a payroll deduction similar to union dues. An employee would be "docked" $3.75 for each hour of work missed.

Careful examination of the wage structures in Tables 5.1 and 5.2 yields a rational explanation for excessive, unwarranted absenteeism. A contractually specified wage structure like that shown in Table 5.1—in which employee benefits are paid regardless of the number of hours the employee works—promotes casual absences in three ways. First, untied (unearned) fringe benefits reduce the *marginal* effective hourly wage rate from $7.75 per hour (Table 5.2, column 3B) to $4 per hour (Table 5.1, column 5). This reduces the price of leisure (that is, absenteeism) and induces the employee to substitute leisure for income—to "buy" more leisure. Thus, the lower marginal effective hourly rate of $4 per hour encourages the employee to be absent from work.

Second, unearned employee benefits constitute a "windfall" transfer of income to the employee because this portion of compensation is not related to hours worked. Therefore, employee demand for "normal" goods will increase and the demand for "inferior" goods will decline. Because leisure is a normal good and work an inferior good, the windfall income transfer created by employee benefits induces the employee to buy more leisure and work fewer hours. Hence, the windfall income effect of unearned employee benefits compounds the absenteeism problem by reinforcing the substitution of leisure for income caused by the lower *marginal* effective hourly wage rate as explained in the previous paragraph.

Table 5.2.

A Comparison of Employee-Benefits-Tied and Employee-Benefits-Untied Wage Structures

	Untied Wage Structure		Tied Wage Structure	
(1) Hours Worked	(2A) Total Weekly Earnings[1]	(3A) Marginal Effective Hourly Wage Rate (Contractual Wage Rate) (Δ col. 2A ÷ Δ col. 1)*	(2B) Total Weekly Earnings[2]	(3B) Marginal Effective Hourly Wage Rate[3] (Δ 2B ÷ Δ col. 1)**
0	$150	$4	$ 0	$7.75
8	182	4	62	7.75
16	214	4	124	7.75
24	246	4	186	7.75
32	278	4	248	7.75
40	310	4	310	7.75
48	358	6[4]	358[6]	6.00
56	422	8[5]	422[7]	8.00

Notes:
1. These figures include the monetary equivalent of employee benefits regardless of the number of hours worked per week—$150.00.
2. These figures include the monetary equivalent of employee benefits only to the extent that work is tendered at a rate of $3.75 per hour worked.
3. These figures are calculated by adding the monetary equivalent of fringe benefits calculated at $3.75 per hour over a scheduled 40-hour workweek to the *nominal* contractual wage rate of $4.00 per hour —that is, $7.75 per hour.
4. This rate is the overtime rate of time and a half—1.5 × $4.00 = $6.00 per hour.
5. This rate is the overtime rate of double time—2.0 × $4.00 = $8.00 per hour.
6. Because the entire value of fringe benefits has been earned at the end of the 40-hour scheduled workweek, this rate is simply the overtime rate of time and a half—1.5 × $4.00 = $6.00 per hour for the 8 hours overtime. Total earnings = $310 + (8 × $6.00)
7. Since the entire value of employee benefits have been earned at the end of the 40-hour scheduled workweek, the rate for the 8 hours overtime is simply the overtime rate of double time—2.0 × $4.00 = $8.00 per hour. Total earnings = $310 + (8 × $6.00) + (8 × $8.00).
* Change in column 2A divided by change in column 1.
** Change in column 2B divided by change in column 1.

Finally, to the degree that the *average* effective hourly wage rate is the controlling factor in the employee "leisure or work" decision-making process, a declining average effective hourly wage rate (see Table 5.1, column 4) caused by employee benefits that are unrelated to hours worked will encourage employee absenteeism by reducing the price of leisure (that is, excessive and unwarranted absenteeism) as the number of hours spent on the job increases. The reduced price of such leisure induces the employee to buy more of this commodity—to be absent from work.

Given an effective wage structure like the one illustrated in Table 5.1 and assuming that an employee knows his or her own tastes and preferences, the employee who abuses sick-leave policies will choose the combination of work and absenteeism that generate the highest level of satisfaction. The employee then selects the specific eight-hour day(s) to be absent, the one(s) consistent with the employee's highest level of satisfaction.

While the more cynical manager may view the previous discussion as support for the deletion of all fringe benefits, such a conclusion is totally unwarranted. Properly tied to hours worked, earned fringe benefits create an incentive to attend regularly by making leisure more expensive. In addition, such benefits as day care centers, medical insurance, and even car pools or company buses reduce absenteeism by eliminating one of its causes: the inability to attend. Indeed, instead of being a part of the problem, these programs can help solve the problem. They are perfectly consistent with effective compensation policies.

The suggested method of direct deduction from employee wages for the costs of unearned fringe benefits may be most effective in those situations where employee benefits are limited to such payments in kind as insurance and pension. There is, however, another approach to this problem where organizations offer employees paid time off, such as vacations, sick leave, holidays, and personal authorized absence in addition to other kinds of employee benefits. It is a well-recognized principle of industrial psychology that adverse behavior modification is best accomplished through corrective action clearly linked to the employee's unwanted behavior. Therefore, the above referenced payback scheme should begin with deductions from the employees paid time off entitlement. In short, after absences surpass some unacceptable threshold number, an employee's paid time off entitlement should be reduced, *quid pro quo*, for additional unauthorized time off prior to cash reimbursement being imposed, prior to an employee being docked monetarily for excessive absences. This clearly links absenteeism control with authorized and paid acceptable absences and makes clear the employer's need for a reliable work force. The current General Motors-United Auto Workers contract[2] utilizes such a mechanism with success.[3] Once the employee reaches 20 percent lost time rate, GM will reduce the paid time off entitlement, on a one-to-one basis, for each additional hour of absence. If the employee continues to be absent, reductions in other fringe benefits are made. Of course, absences beyond the employee's control, such as serious injuries, will not be used against the worker to reduce his or her benefits. The determination of whether an absence should be excused for purposes of benefit reductions is made by a joint UAW-GM committee.

Further variations on this theme, such as replacement of absentee days through increasing required service for pension eligibility or reductions in pension benefits, are also possible. Whatever the adjustment mechanism, the important fact is that workers not be permitted to drive up their effective hourly wage rate by simply failing to report for work. Piece rates and task rates contain built-in adjustment mechanisms. On the other hand, the incomes of salaried employees require adjustment in the same fashion as the fringe benefits of the previous analysis since salaries are not directly tied to actual hours worked. A more indepth discussion of salaries follows.

White Collar Employees

White collar employees are a somewhat different absenteeism problem than blue collar workers. White collar employees may be categorized into two groups for present purposes: professional and technical employees and managerial employees. Both groups are highly visible to blue collar employees and their attendance behavior will have an impact on the blue collar group. Possibly more important, the incentives of white collar employees are often more difficult to identify and examine than those of blue collar workers. To the extent that white collar employees are motivated by economic items such as fringe benefits, salaries, and wages, the prior discussion concerning effective wage rates applies. But the incentives for the white collar group are more interrelated and complex than the foregoing analysis implies. For this reason, it is appropriate to examine these employees.

Professional and Technical Employees

In any white or blue collar employment, it is necessary to create an efficient and equitable compensation program. Yet these employees pose a significant problem for purposes of determining appropriate compensation policies. Nontraditional compensation important to professional and technical employees includes in-service refresher training, receipt of scientific or professional literature, and travel expenses and fees for professional meetings and seminars. Not only are these items regarded as compensation by employees, but they are absolutely critical for maintenance of professional competence. No one would seriously consider adjusting such benefits, *quid pro quo*, for excessive absence. To do so would be tantamount to "cutting your nose off to spite your face." In general, this group of employees should be handled in much the same manner as blue collar workers—paying strict attention to different aspects of compensation where these can be manipulated without adversely affecting the quality of labor provided. For example, it is preferable to withhold vacation time, or to use direct payback for absences among professional and technical workers instead of "in kind" payments. Indeed, attempting to correct absenteeism problems by reducing in kind payments that are designed to maintain or enhance professional competence penalizes the organization rather than the absentee.

Managerial Employees

Supervisory personnel are typically subject to the same economic incentives as blue collar workers. Yet two interesting aspects of compensation and absenteeism control should be noted. First, supervisor rewards are generally tied to output, sales, or some other tangible measure of profits or production. These personnel are rarely rewarded for maintaining good human relations, low absenteeism rates in their departments, or effective labor relations; yet absenteeism control, good morale, and reduced grievance problems are essential to greater worker productivity. Supervisory compensation such as profit sharing, merit raises, and bonuses could easily be structured to give these personnel a greater incentive (which is readily identified with absenteeism control) to be more effective managers. This is a simple compensation policy concept that is largely ignored in most organizations—tie rewards to performance. The reduction of human relations problems, grievances, and absenteeism is an appropriate managerial activity. It should be evaluated with good performance rewarded and poor performance corrected.

The second issue involves the use of salaries as method of compensation. Managerial personnel, as well as many professional and technical employees, are compensated on the basis of a salary. Salaries are not tied to the hours or days of work and are typically based on the week or month. Salaries, therefore, hide the fact that hours of work are what is often expected. Again, the fringe benefit analysis applies; if the salary is not tied to hours of work, the effective hourly wage may be driven up by simply being absent from work. Appropriate performance evaluation must be utilized and compensation based on output where appropriate and tied to the hours of work where proper. A college professor employed by a nationally prestigious research institution provides an excellent example. If published research is the primary responsibility of the position, it is logical to examine the quality and quantity of the professor's research output rather than time spent in the classroom or office. On the other hand, if teaching is his primary job responsibility, the professor's classroom attendance and office accessibility become the appropriate factors for performance evaluation.

Before proceeding, it is interesting to note that the analysis has focused on hours of work. This is important since the problem at hand is absenteeism. Output during those hours of work is yet another often separate problem that will affect overall productivity. Yet if employees are regular in attendance, productivity should increase due to fewer replacement workers being needed, better morale, and reduced need to use less qualified employees as fill-ins. With managerial employees, the organization will find that better control is achieved when recourse to replacement of temporary supervisors is not as frequent when the ranks of experienced management are not thinned by high rates of absenteeism.

QUALITY OF WORK ENVIRONMENT

Closely related to economic incentives is the quality of the work environment. Economic incentives are powerful managerial tools. However, it is important to remember that employees will react to other incentives as well. From the discussion in the first chapter, you will recall that worker alienation was pointed out as an important source of absenteeism. The purpose of this portion of the absenteeism control program is to point out how alienation can be minimized, if not eliminated, and to suggest methods for making the work environment more conducive to regular employee work attendance. Alienation, as used here, refers to an employee's deliberate choice to not attend work or be a productive member of the organization. Alienation, therefore, is the voluntary decision not to attend work for other than economic reasons.

The Elimination or Minimization of Alienation

Three main causes of worker alienation are observed in organization: poor human relations, poor physical environment, and worker self-actualization difficulties. The minimization or elimination of these sources of alienation are important to an organization's overall absentee-control policy.[4]

Human Relations

An appropriate human relations policy is important to the effective operation of all organizations. This is especially true in organizations comprising people with varied backgrounds as well as differing responsibilities. An employee who finds it difficult to get along with the boss or co-workers will be more apt to be an absenteeism problem than those workers who get along. The worker who becomes alienated from his or her supervisor or co-workers may not only be absent from work but may also exhibit other symptoms of alienation, such as being argumentative (even insubordinate), filing frequent and often trivial grievances, reducing his or her level of productivity, and withdrawing socially from the work group. Although the symptoms are easily spotted, the underlying causes are more difficult to diagnose. Alcoholics, drug abusers, or those suffering traumatic difficulties in their personal lives may exhibit essentially the same type of behaviors. It is, therefore, important that supervisors be trained to spot individuals exhibiting such symptoms and attempt to ascertain the nature and cause of the employee's problem. Too often first line supervisory personnel, even those with years of experience and substantial human relations training, will be unable to identify either the likely cause of the symptomatic behavior or its complete nature. This is why it is important to have a human relations specialist or, in cases of larger operations, a human relations department. The purpose of these departments is to assist the employee with his or her problem. The most common type of department in industry today is that concerned with alcohol or drug rehabilitation. While these programs are necessary, they should not be the only programs offered, nor should they be billed as the centerpiece of the overall human relations effort. If employees believe that alcohol and drug rehabilitation are the sole services provided by the human relations department, they will often avoid contact with it to avoid any stigma that management and co-workers may attach to the use of such services.

The human relations department should offer a wide range of services. Not only should drug and alcohol rehabilitation services be provided, but workplace and personal counselling referral services are valuable and should also be offered. First, the notion that a human relations department is involved primarily with drugs and alcohol is dispelled. Second, many other human problems can and do have the same devastating impact on worker reliability and productivity. Services such as family counselling, retirement counselling, financial planning, health referrals and assistance, car-pooling information, day care referrals (and in some cases even day care centers), safety training, and dozens of other such programs have been successfully implemented. Eli Lilly, for example, has successfully used such programs to prevent the development of absenteeism problems. The United States Postal Service, on the other hand, has had some degree of success with these programs in correcting absenteeism problems once they have occurred and have been identified.

The skeptic might question both the value and the affordability of such programs. Granted, a crew of industrial psychologists, financial planners, bus drivers, physicians (even part time), retirement advisers, and baby sitters are not cheap, but even such an impressive array of human relations personnel could very well prove to be a financial bargain for very large organizations that suffer the problems that this approach could solve. For organizations smaller than General Motors, ITT, and the postal service, a more realistic approach may be to have in-house personnel capable of referring employees to the services already provided in the community. If problems are more frequent and can be handled internally with better control and still remain economical, such staff should be employed.

Finally, it must be remembered that a human relations staff department cannot substitute for good managerial human relations skills. Supervisory personnel must not only possess technical skills but must also possess the personal characteristics and values that allow a person to be an effective manager. There are no good substitutes for honesty, good communications skills, fairness, firmness, and good judgment. Often, the personal traits of an individual will make it easier or more difficult to acquire these skills, but training to improve such skills often proves valuable. Additionally, supervisors must be advised as to what is expected of them and rewarded or punished accordingly, particularly stressing achievements or lack thereof in human relations activities. Too often, the human relations portion of the supervisory function is ignored in goal setting, incentive structures, and disciplinary policies. Since supervisors take their cues from official policy as manifest through organizational goals, incentives, and disciplinary regulations, so too will supervisors also ignore this area in favor of a more concentrated effort on other details of supervision. Since supervisors tend to be pragmatic and somewhat short sighted, the longer-run problems associated with failures in human relations tend to be ignored unless the firm's personnel program requires and upper management focuses on good human relations.

Supervisors do not necessarily need to be extroverts or overly friendly types. In fact, such characteristics make for popularity and not necessarily good supervision. The appropriate goal is to minimize personality conflicts and other types of interpersonal difficulties. From this perspective, a "fair but firm" demeanor is probably the best model for effective management. A supervisory philosophy of fairness and firmness may be the single most important element—the cornerstone—of a human relations program that reduces worker alienation and, thus, absenteeism. More concerning this managerial approach will be presented in the final section of this chapter.

Poor Physical Environment

When one thinks of quality of work life, often one of the first things to come to mind is the physical environment. Alienation and its associated problems are often related to the quality of the physical environment. There are three dimensions to be considered with the physical work environment: health and safety, physical comfort, and esthetics. The control of each of these factors is dependent on the type of activity the organization is involved in. Therefore, the following discussion can only be viewed as a general guideline and not a specific formula for all organizations.

Health and safety issues are subject to statutory regulations in most work places. Obviously, injuries and illnesses directly influence employee attendance behavior. An unsafe or unhealthy work environment or an uncaring managerial attitude toward health and safety issues will beget worker alienation which, in turn, begets absenteeism. In cases where management meets the minimum standards of the Occupational Safety and Health Act (OSHA) but is openly hostile toward them and the agency charged with their enforcement, workers may construe this hostility as evidence that management is hardened and callous. Public statements or statements to the work force concerning such regulations should be well thought out and kept to a minimum where possible.

Since injury and illness are important causes of absenteeism, preventative measures often pay for themselves directly and very quickly. An on-the-job injury should precipitate a prompt and thorough investigation by management not only to prevent reoccurrences of the injury but to demonstrate to the work force that management is concerned with health and safety issues and will take appropriate measures to ensure a healthy and safe work environment.

One of the worst approaches to health and safety is epitomized by the practices of a major manufacturing firm with facilities throughout the United States. This firm has a very visible safety campaign utilizing pocket protectors with safety slogans, posters, pep talks, and other gimmicks, but is consistently found in violation of minimum OSHA standards. The employees might rightly ask: "Where's the program's substance?" In addition, discipline is automatic for any employee who is injured on the job—regardless of the circumstances. When injuries occur, investigations are rare, and subsequent corrective action is almost nonexistent. The result is that management has created an atmosphere of fear and has undermined its credibility concerning safety-related issues. Correction of worker alienation will demand implementation of a safety campaign directed toward substantive safety issues and less toward propaganda—toward the investigation and correction of safety problems, toward strict compliance with

OSHA standards, and toward the elimination of the automatic assessment of discipline for each and every safety rule infraction regardless of the degree of fault on the part of the employee. Otherwise, alienation will continue with its attendant absenteeism problems.

Improving the worker's physical comfort as well as the overall esthetics of the work environment are also important ways of reducing alienation and motivating employees to attend work. Unfortunately, many of the occupations most in need of improved esthetics do not readily lend themselves to such improvement. Coal mining, foundry work, and meat packing are but a few examples of such activities. Even in these industries, however, there are still some things that can be done to make the work environment more pleasant. Employee break rooms or lounges could be provided, and restrooms should be kept clean and made as attractive and pleasant as possible. If employees are given clean, pleasant surroundings for breaks and lunch periods even though the immediate work environment can be only marginally improved, management will have demonstrated its concern which, in itself, should reduce alienation and improve worker attendance.

The science of ergonomics has much to offer laboratories, manufacturing facilities, offices, and other firms interested in creating a more pleasant work environment and reducing worker alienation. As such, it is an important weapon in management's arsenal for controlling absenteeism. Pleasant and clean working conditions, work stations designed for people to work comfortably, and good climate control not only increase productivity but help reduce alienation, thereby motivating employees to come to work. The use of ergonomics and the conscious attempt by management to create a clean, comfortable, and pleasant workplace will demonstrate to employees management's concern and go a long way toward reducing any unpleasant aspects of work due to the work environment itself.

Self-Actualization

Self-actualization is concerned with fulfilling one's perceived potential, desires, or needs. It is often presumed by management that self-actualization is a problem characteristic of white collar employees rather than blue collar workers, but both categories of workers are subject to this type of problem. Problems of self-actualization can result in alienation and, thus, absenteeism when employees do not feel they are being given an opportunity to advance or are not rewarded on the basis of their relative merit. While this particular source of absenteeism is often the most difficult to diagnose, it is the easiest and generally least costly to correct. If left uncorrected, however, self-actualization problems cannot only become serious sources of absenteeism but also of high turnover rates, poor morale, and even legal difficulties. The most obvious self-actualization problems are created by such things as nepotism, "blanket" salary schedules, poor evaluation procedures, and race or sex discrimination. Many firms and other types of organizations have policies that prohibit nepotism—the preferential treatment of sons, daughters, nephews, and nieces of present employees. Such a policy declaration, even for relatively small organizations, is well advised (a notable exception being purely family owned and operated businesses with virtually no hired career-oriented help). Otherwise, whether justified or not, employees will presume the worst, thereby precluding an unemotional and rational evaluation of the performance of family members and other employees as well. This development is precisely the type of situation that the firm but fair philosophy of management is intended to prevent. Preferential treatment of relatives breeds jealousy and discord. On the other hand, hiring relatives and holding them to stricter standards for promotion and pay increases will also lead employees to question the basic fairness of management. In short, nepotism constitutes a "catch–22" for management; it is best avoided.

Blanket salary steps or salary schedules are a symptom of either a lazy or ill-informed management. If productivity, efficiency, and merit are valued by the organization, it will be evident in that organization's compensation program. A simple rule of thumb with compensation programs is "you get what you pay for." If merit determinations are not fairly and consistently made, you cannot expect people to provide meritorious service, and unless merit is the basis of compensation, you cannot expect continued meritorious service. The problem, therefore, is reduced to one of appropriate measurement of merit and appropriate employee feedback when merit is found to be wanting. The second aspect of the problem is the easiest to resolve. It takes, for want of a better name, "intestinal fortitude." Unpleasant tasks are a part of the territory for a manager. It is never easy to tell someone that he or she is not performing adequately or, worse yet, to fire someone. When positive feedback is warranted, however, the manager should discharge his or her responsibility and provide the necessary feedback. Managerial evaluation of employees and communication of same to employees must occur on a regular basis. However, it should never become so institutionalized and mechanistic that it loses its importance and meaning to employees. Therefore, the best approach may very well be effective communication training combined with appropriate organization policies requiring periodic and specific types of feedback. Evaluation, itself, however, is not quite so simple. Evaluation of performance must be job specific, valid, and reliable. If managers have a specific goal to accomplish, the appropriate evaluation instrument is goal accomplishment—the degree to which the goal has been achieved. In structuring the evaluation process, it must be remembered that the evaluation of merit, by nature, tends to be highly subjective. Consequently, the more objective and rational the evaluation, the better feedback it will provide and the more likely it is to form the basis for an effective compensation policy.

Since evaluation is a complicated process and job specific, organizations are well advised to procure the services of an expert in the field. The evaluation process should not be so complicated after it is in place to reduce its understandability or require so much time and effort that it will not be used. A trained expert can generally structure a valid and reliable evaluation process that is readily understood and requires only a few hours per evaluated employee. Unless the process is utilized effectively at appropriate points in time, the evaluation of performance is a meaningless exercise.

Self-actualization consists of self-evaluation relative to others in a selected group. As a result, individual perceptions are the key features of this process. Even in cases where evaluation feedback is good, nepotism and other forms of discrimination nonexistent, and the compensation program properly structured to account for merit, some workers may still feel they have not been properly compensated or given fair opportunities for advancement. In some cases, these employees may be justified in their criticism. For example, take the case of a firm with a disproportionately large number of positions at a specific level that leaves few opportunities for advancement. Here, bottlenecks of quality personnel are created. To avoid this type of self-actualization problem, opportunities for lateral transfer or retraining must be provided. This problem is not unique to blue collar occupations. Where encountered, employees compare their progress to a wide range of persons within and outside their own occupation and organization.

Those workers who incorrectly assess their own merit and potential are of particular concern. The problem can often be corrected through appropriate evaluation feedback. Where feedback fails, other corrective measures also normally fail. Hence, the old proverb that "an ounce of prevention is worth a pound of cure" applies to self-actualization problems. Careful screening and career planning is often the best—the only—approach; yet many organizations make little or no effort in this area. If employees' qualifications and ambitions are carefully matched to vacant positions, many self-actualization problems can be prevented. Needless to say, egotists and chronic complainers should be avoided since they are "a self-actualization problem waiting to happen." Once it does, it can spread in epidemic fashion to other employees. This can happen several ways. Egotists are quick to point out their own accomplishments as well as their co-workers' failures. This behavior creates self-actualization problems for their fellow workers. Chronic complainers create the impression that there are a greater number of deficiencies in the work environment than actually do exist. This too creates job dissatisfaction and its attendant problems. In short, both egotists and chronic complainers poison the work environment; they increase the costs to other employees of coming to work. This begets job dissatisfaction that generates more complaints and higher rates of absenteeism.

It is worth noting that personal problems may also become self-actualization problems. Drug abusers, alcoholics, the chronically ill, and those experiencing family problems are commonly unable to leave their problems at home. At work, these problems manifest themselves as problems of self-actualization. Consequently, the human relations approach discussed above is best suited to correct this type of self-actualization problem.

The foregoing paragraphs have focused upon the concept of alienation. As defined here, alienation is an employee's unwillingness to become involved in or feel a part of the organization; absenteeism is often the result. It is important, therefore, to make employees at all levels of the organization feel that they are productive and are a needed part of the organization. Many times this can be accomplished simply by listening to the employees, regardless of the manner through which the message is conveyed (for example, suggestion boxes, informal meetings with foremen, formal meetings with upper echelon management, and so on). The important thing is that the employee feel needed and wanted; that the employee sense that the organization needs the employee in much the same way that a plant needs water. One of the true marks of a good manager is the ability to listen to and learn from employees. Likewise, one sure sign of a good management team is its ability to integrate all workers into the organization, thereby eliminating alienation and its attendant problems.

DISCIPLINE

One of the most unpleasant tasks of any supervisory position is the assessment of discipline. It has been the authors' experience that the administration of discipline is poorly handled by a surprisingly large number of firms. Although discipline, its purpose, and its proper administration constitute the subject matter of a later chapter, a few remarks are in order here.

The focal point of this chapter has been employee motivation and the proper ordering of economic, social, and psychological incentives. There is, however, another category of corrective actions called discipline or "negative behavioral strategies." Unlike positive behavioral strategies that attempt to elicit desirable behavior through systems of reward, negative behavioral strategies attempt to discourage unwanted behavior by punishing it, that is, through the assessment of discipline. The basic theory behind discipline is best summarized by the "hot stove principle"—a person touches a hot stove, gets burned, and learns not to touch hot stoves. To be effective (that is, to discourage unwanted behavior), discipline must be administered in accord with several basic principles: that discipline only be assessed for just cause (that employee behavior warrant discipline); that penalties be promptly assessed to indicate clearly the connection between unwanted behavior and attendant discipline; that the severity of any penalty be in proportion to the severity of the offense, for example, an employee's first absence does not warrant discharge (by the same token, the physical assault of a supervisor warrants more than a verbal reprimand); that employees be clearly informed of all shop disciplinary and safety rules; and that discipline be administered and enforced in a consistent, objective, dispassionate, and evenhanded fashion.

Discipline for absenteeism must also be corrective or progressive in nature. Arbitrators as well as the courts have not hesitated to overturn discipline where employers have failed to point out to the offending worker the error of his or her ways and to attempt to remedy the wrongful behavior, where infractions recur in some pattern, are habitual, and pose no serious immediate threat to other workers or to the organization itself. A certain number of employee absences is to be expected. Everyone will be absent on occasion. Managers should excuse such absences due, for example, to occasional bouts with the flu. Discipline should be reserved for absences that have become habitual and disruptive—excessive—in nature. Consequently, employee termination for the first instance of absence is not appropriate or corrective and will not be sustained either by arbitrators or the courts.

Once an employee's absences reach an unacceptable level, a common procedure in the assessment of discipline in absenteeism cases is for the labor agreement or personnel policy to specify a definite progression of steps, each successive step involving a progressively more severe penalty up to and including termination (for example, oral warning, written warning, suspension, and termination). Although the point at which absences become unacceptable, the number of disciplinary steps, and the exact progression in the severity of penalties may differ from one labor-management relationship to the next, there should be one constant—the message conveyed to the employee, namely, that absenteeism is unacceptable behavior and, if uncorrected, will culminate in termination.

There are times when management may believe circumstances warrant a more lenient penalty or no penalty at all for absenteeism. Management would be well advised to exercise managerial leniency judiciously in accord with predetermined criteria for its use in order to avoid employee or union claims that management's action was disparate, arbitrary, and capricious. If such claims are found to be meritorious, arbitrators and the courts will disturb any discipline based thereon. Besides the spectre of arbitral reversal, an even more important consideration is that disciplinary inconsistency creates fear and breeds contempt on the part of employees for managerially determined rules and regulations, further hampering the achievement of traditional management goals.

These and other discipline-related issues will be discussed in greater detail in Chapter 8.

SUMMARY OF THE ABSENTEEISM CONTROL PROGRAM

Absenteeism is a multidimensional problem and the program suggested herein is an integrative approach to absenteeism control. Its major points are outlined below:

1. Compensation programs should be tied to hours of work (or other appropriate output measure) so as to prevent employees from increasing their effective hourly wage by absenting themelves from work.

2. A human relations program should be instituted to either correct or refer employees

to corrective services for various personal problems affecting, among other things, attendance behavior.

3. Human relations training should be made available for supervisors to ensure that supervisor-employee relations do not alienate employees thereby causing absenteeism.

4. Responsible and effective health and safety programs directly reduce absenteeism due to illness and injury and indirectly reduce absenteeism by showing managerial concern and commitment to providing a healthy and safe work environment.

5. The physical environment must be as clean, pleasant, and comfortable as is practical given the nature of the organization; this reduces the unpleasant nature of many work activities therefore reducing alienation and thus absenteeism.

6. Appropriate applicant screening and career planning is necessary to match applicants properly with vacant jobs and to prevent future self-actualization problems.

7. Promotions, merit raises, and lateral transfers should be used to reward meritorious service and prevent quality employees from being locked in to lower level positions.

8. Feedback, both positive and negative, must be given employees at appropriate times to reinforce quality work and correct employee deficiencies.

9. Supervisors must be given incentives to perform effectively in human relations, communications, evaluation, and disciplinary matters.

10. An effective, valid, and reliable yet simple evaluation program must be initiated and used to ensure merit is recognized and rewarded as well as poor performance corrected.

11. An effective disciplinary program must be initiated and appropriately administered to correct absentee behavior and remove employee discretion concerning their attendance.

These basic components are based on the following prerequisites.

12. Appropriate data on absenteeism is gathered and monitored to ascertain the causes, frequency, and duration of employee absences to allow for appropriate policy measures and to determine their effectiveness.

13. Management must adopt a guiding philosophy of fair but firm personnel administration to facilitate the implementation of the proposed absenteeism control policy.

14. The program (or the portions adopted) must be molded or fine tuned to the specific organization and activity in which it is going to be applied and not blindly adopted without consideration for the specific situations it will be functioning in.

NOTES

1. The authors found this to be true in the case of the "Agreement between General Motors Corporation and the UAW" for 1976 and 1979. The costs of absenteeism to General Motors Corporation and the way in which the labor agreement and its administration operated to produce these absenteeism-related costs are examined in Chapter 6.

2. See Appendix.

3. Marjorie Sorge, "New Programs Slash Absenteeism," *Automotive News* (October 10, 1983):3; "Labor Letter," *Wall Street Journal* (March 19, 1985):1; "The No-Shows," *Forbes* (April 8, 1985):10.

4. Methods of eliminating or minimizing various sources of alienation are explored in Chapter 7.

Applying the Integrated Approach to Absenteeism Control: The Case of General Motors

6

Whether you work by the piece
Or work by the day
Decreasing the hours
Increases the pay.

Mrs. Ira Steward

As emphasized throughout this volume, absenteeism is a problem of increasing concern to management and organized labor alike. Nowhere was the magnitude of this problem more apparent than in the economically ailing automobile industry of a few years ago—an economic setback from which the industry has yet to fully recover. Declining sales, stiff foreign competition, industry-wide worker layoffs, and the financial problems of Chrysler Corporation had combined to underscore the need for increased efficiency and productivity. A necessary first step toward achieving this goal was the elimination of excessive absenteeism.

At that time, the authors spent some time with General Motors Corporation, exploring its patterns of excessive absences in light of the provisions of the contract between the company and the United Auto Workers and made an interesting discovery. It appeared that excessive absenteeism was simply rational employee response to contractually structured and/or administered incentives to stay away from the job. The specifics of that investigation follow. Although General Motors was the focus of the study, the examination of the costs of, the factors responsible for, and methods of reducing excessive absenteeism are generally applicable to other enterprises as detailed in the previous chapters of this book.

The material contained herein was first published as: Clarence R. Deitsch and David A. Dilts, "Getting Absent Workers Back on the Job: The Case of General Motors," *Business Horizons* (September/October 1981) 24:52–58. Copyright 1981 by the Foundation for the School of Business at Indiana University. Reprinted by permission.

THE COSTS OF ABSENTEEISM

General Motors Corporation and the United Automobile Workers contractually authorize a 5 percent absenteeism rate. This rate has been negotiated in the form of paid holidays, paid personal absences, paid vacations, and paid personal holidays.[1] The cost of contractually authorized time away from work has presumably been accepted by management and labor as a form of employee compensation. However, the rate of casual absenteeism, resulting from the failure of employees to report to work as scheduled, is equal to that of contractually authorized time off–5 percent.[2] Casual absences constitute the heart of the absenteeism problem.

General Motors Corporation normally employs approximately 500,000 members of the United Automobile Workers Union. The average union member employed by General Motors earns $10 per hour. Fringe benefits, prorated over a standard 40 hour work week, amount to an additional $5 per hour. The fringe benefit component of the compensation package is paid regardless of whether or not an employee reports for work.[3]

The 5 percent casual absenteeism rate translates into 25,000 employee absences each scheduled work day.[4] Given 250 scheduled work days annually, absenteeism claims 6,250,000 work days or 50 million hours each year. Each hour lost to absenteeism costs General Motors $20–$5 in contractually guaranteed fringe benefits paid to the absent worker and $15 in compensation paid to the absent worker's replacement. The total annual cost of casual absenteeism amounts to $1 billion.[5]

The national rate of absenteeism due to acute illness was 1.38 percent in 1977.[6] Initially, it might appear that absenteeism at General Motors is four times the national average or that excessive absenteeism amounted to 3.62 percent, the difference between the national rate and the General Motors rate. If it were not for the fact that the contract provides for a 5 percent authorized absenteeism rate, the above observation would be technically correct. However, since a cogent argument can be made that contractually authorized time away from work makes adequate provision for absences due to acute illness, all casual absences that occur at General Motors can properly be termed "excessive absences." Hence, excessive absenteeism costs amount to $1 billion annually.

Although explicit costs are substantial, the true costs of excessive absenteeism are much greater than $1 billion.[7] Absences are not spread evenly over the scheduled work week, over the year, or over the work force. The absenteeism rate increases significantly on the first and the last days of the scheduled work week and during certain seasons of the year. This cyclical pattern of absenteeism increases maintenance and production scheduling costs and leads to increased quality control problems. Further, since 85 percent of all casual absences are due to erratic job attendance by 10 percent of the work force, a morale problem is created among employees with good attendance records, which adversely affects overall worker productivity. Our discussion of casual absenteeism, however, will deal only with explicit costs since the data necessary for calculating implicit costs are either not collected or are not generally available due to their highly sensitive nature. Remember, though, that the total costs of casual absenteeism are much higher than the explicit costs.

The burden of casual absenteeism is borne to a greater or lesser extent by three not necessarily different groups of individuals: General Motors' customers, stockholders, and employees with good attendance records. Customers share the burden to the extent that automobile prices reflect the higher labor costs associated with casual absences. Shareholders expend between $250 million and $1 billion annually for services not rendered. The $250-million figure would apply if casual absences occurred evenly over 250 scheduled work days; nonproductive expenditures would approach $1 billion the greater the degree of cyclical concentration of casual absences.[8] Maintaining a superfluous work force of 25,000 employees to cover casual absences during concentrated peaks of absenteeism adds approximately $750 million to nonproductive expenditures.[9]

The burden of casual absenteeism upon workers with exemplary attendance records is particularly onerous. These workers subsidize workers with poor work habits. If the attendance record of the 10 percent of the work force responsible for 85 percent of all absences was simply brought into line with that of the 90 percent of the work force with good work habits, casual absenteeism would decline from 5 percent to .83 percent. The work force could be reduced by 20,850 workers, the number of employees formerly used as replacements for casual absentees. Cost savings, depending upon the previous cyclical pattern of casual absences, would range from $209 to $834 million.[10] Distributed across the board to employees with good attendance records, the savings would provide hourly wage rate increases ranging from .22 cents to .87 cents per hour. The subsidy would be greater if casual absenteeism were entirely eliminated.

RATIONALE FOR ABSENTEEISM

The jingle, written by the wife of Ira Steward, the leader of the eight-hour day movement, and quoted at the beginning of this chapter, aptly summarizes two of the historical goals of organized labor: shorter hours and higher hourly rates of pay.[11] These goals have become so pervasive that they permeate the current effective hourly wage structures of many firms. The following table indicates effective hourly wage rates paid to General Motors' employees for different amounts of time spent on the job. Although the nominal hourly wage rate remains constant at $10 per hour up to 40 hours, the effective hourly wage rate declines over the work week until additional hours worked at overtime premiums pull the effective wage rate back up. This pattern results from the fixed component of compensation: fringe benefits in the amount of $230 per week are paid regardless of the number of hours worked. Herein lies the cause of excessive absenteeism. Whereas explanations of absenteeism offered in the body of literature treating this topic range from employee laziness to worker disenchantment, we suggest that casual absences are due to the workers' realization that neither the contract nor its administration penalizes them for taking excessive time off.[12]

The following figure depicts the response of a typical absentee to the wage structure shown in the table. Curves I_1 and I_2 show all combinations of income and leisure that yield the same level of satisfaction. In the absence of any other information, the employee is indifferent as to which combination is chosen, except that all points along I_2 are preferred to all points along I_1 because combinations along I_2 represent greater quantities of income or leisure.

The line from A to F depicts the total weekly earnings (including the monetary equivalent of fringe benefits) of the employee as provided by the General Motors–United Automobile Workers contract for different hours worked per week. The slope of line AF is the marginal effective hourly wage rate ($10 per hour) under the contract. This wage rate can also be thought of as the price of absenteeism (that is, leisure) per hour. Distance OA measures the amount of fringe benefits ($230) authorized by the contract regardless of the number of hours worked or taken as leisure. As the figure illustrates, the employee selects point E, working 32 hours, earning $550 in income, and taking 8 hours of lei-

Table 6.1.
General Motors: Average Effective Hourly Wage Rates Inclusive of Fringe Benefits and Exclusive of Contractually Authorized Paid Absences

Hours Worked	Total Weekly Earnings[1]	Earnings Per 8 Hours Worked	Average Effective Hourly Wage Rate (Total weekly earnings/ Hours worked)	Marginal Effective Hourly Wage Rate (Δ Total weekly earnings/ Δ Hours worked)
0	$230[2]	–	∞	$10
8	310	$80	$38.75	10
16	390	80	24.38	10
24	470	80	19.58	10
32	550	80	17.19	10
40	630	80	15.75[2]	10
48	750[3]	120	15.63	15
56	910[4]	160	16.25	20

1. These figures include the monetary equivalent of fringe benefits—$230/wk.
2. Although fringe benefits cost General Motors $200/wk per worker or $5.00/hr pro-rated over a scheduled 40 hr. week, the taxable monetary equivalents for the average employee are, respectively, $230/wk and $5.75/hr. Hence, for 40 hours worked, the average effective wage rate is $15.75 (i.e., $10/hr + $5.75/hr.).
3. This figure is calculated based upon 40 hours at the straight-time nominal wage of $10/hr., 8 hours at time and a half ($15/hr.), and fringe benefits of $230.
4. This figure is calculated based upon 40 hours at $10/hr., 8 hours at time and a half ($15/hr.), 8 hours at double time ($20/hr.), plus fringe benefits of $230.

Figure 6.1.
Leisure/Work Choice of a Typical Absentee

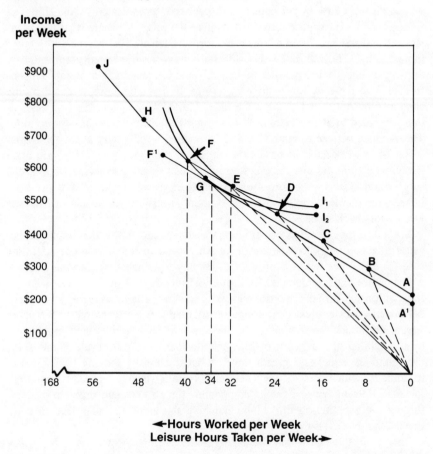

Income per Week

← Hours Worked per Week
Leisure Hours Taken per Week →

sure. The employee voluntarily chooses to be absent from work 8 hours each week.

Line OF illustrates total weekly earnings of the same employee under a wage structure where the value of fringe benefits is tied directly to the number of hours worked. The employee qualifies for the full value of fringe benefits only on the completion of 40 hours of work. The slope of line OF is the new marginal effective hourly wage rate of $15.75 per hour ($10 per hour wage + $5.75 per hour in fringe benefits). This modified wage structure induces the employee to select point F, working 40 hours, earning $630 in income, and taking only those hours of leisure that are contractually authorized. Casual absenteeism is not a problem.

As is immediately apparent from the figure, the contractually specified wage structure promotes casual absences. Specifically, payment of fringe benefits in an amount unrelated to the number of hours worked creates the absenteeism problem in three ways.[13] First, fringe benefits reduce the marginal effective hourly wage rate from $15.75 per hour to $10 per hour, as indicated by the slopes of lines OF and AF, respectively. This reduces the price of leisure (that is, absenteeism) and induces the employee to substitute leisure for income—to "buy" more leisure. The impact of this substitution can be illustrated graphically by drawing a line, A^1F^1, parallel to line AF and tangent to I_1 at point G. Confronted with the now lower price of leisure, $10 per hour, represented by the slope of line A^1F^1, and at the same time, limited to the same level of satisfaction generated by the original choice of point F, the employee chooses point G. The distance between points F and G, measured horizontally along the hours-worked-per-week axis, identifies the impact of the lower price of leisure upon the number of hours that the employee chooses to work each week (that is, the substitution effect). The lower marginal effective wage rate of $10 per hour induces the employee to choose only 6 hours of leisure—to be absent from the job 6 hours each week.

Second, fringe benefits constitute a transfer of income to the employee because this portion of compensation is not related to hours worked. As is the case for any other increase in income, employee demand for "normal" goods will increase and the demand for "inferior" goods will decline. Since leisure falls within the former category and work within the latter category, the windfall income transfer created by fringe benefits induces the employee to buy more leisure and work fewer hours. The income transfer is represented graphically by the parallel upward shift of line A^1F^1 to line AF. As a result of this shift, the employee achieves a greater level of satisfaction by moving from point G to point E, with hours of work declining from 34 to 32. Hence, the windfall income effect of fringe benefits compounds the absenteeism problem by reinforcing the substitution effect—by inducing the employee to select an additional 2 hours of leisure.

Finally, to the extent that the average effective hourly wage rate is the key variable in understanding the leisure or work decision, a declining average effective hourly wage rate, which is caused by fringe benefits that are unrelated to hours worked, will encourage employee absenteeism by reducing the price of leisure (absenteeism) as the number of hours spent on the job increases.[14] The reduced price of leisure induces the employee to buy more of this commodity—to be absent from work.

Given an effective wage structure similar to the one negotiated by General Motors Corporation and the United Automobile Workers, and assuming that an employee knows his or her own tastes and preferences, each employee will choose the combination of work and absenteeism that generates the highest level of satisfaction. The employee then selects the specific eight-hour shift(s) to miss in accordance with the employee's highest level of satisfaction.

The employee's ability to select additional leisure beyond the contractually authorized amount has not been limited through contract administration. Contract provisions governing the administration of discipline, particularly those addressing the problem of absenteeism, have not been enforced. Contract administration by General Motors has increasingly been characterized by the propensity to exchange strict enforcement of disciplinary contract provisions relating to absenteeism for greater management flexibility in other contract areas perceived as generating short-term monetary payoffs—for example, in the area of work assignment and scheduling. This practice, however, is not limited to General Motors. Concern has recently surfaced regarding the impact upon long-run, firm profitability of the widely adopted corporate policy of evaluating managerial personnel according to short-run criteria and then rewarding managers through promotional transfer. Promotion accompanied by transfer—"hop-scotching" as the practice has been appropriately termed—eliminates long-run managerial accountability and responsibility.[15] Absenteeism falls into that category of long-term problems that are often overlooked.

Whatever the rationale for nonenforcement of disciplinary contract provisions addressing the problem of absenteeism, the result is the same: first-line supervisors, consistently undermined by mid- and upper-level management at the later stages of grievance procedure, become reluctant to write up disciplinary cases involving absenteeism and eventually ignore the problem altogether. By the same token, employees soon come to realize that there are no penalties for casual absences. In short, contract administration facilitates rational employee response to contractually structured incentives for casual absences by removing attendant personal costs. This combination of factors permits the employee to achieve a higher level of satisfaction than otherwise possible under the intended terms and conditions of the contract—an increase in satisfaction represented by the difference between curves I_1 and I_2 in the above figure.

POLICY IMPLICATIONS

The need to alleviate the casual absenteeism problem is highlighted by the significant costs it imposes upon other employees, customers, and shareholders. Given the factors responsible for the problem, several remedies become immediately apparent:

• Removal of compensation-related incentives for casual absences. Direct tying of fringe benefits to straight-time hours worked increases the cost to the employee for time spent away from the job. The cost could be assessed through payroll deductions similar to the "check-off." In the case of General Motors, each hour of unauthorized absence would result in a $5.00 payroll deduction.

• Adherence to the contractually specified disciplinary procedure and enforcement of contractually prescribed disciplinary penalties. Chronic absenteeism by a relatively small segment of the work force reflects either a poorly structured or poorly administered disciplinary procedure. Whatever the shortcoming(s) of the procedure, the intended corrective impact has not been achieved. Reduction and elimination of casual absences requires a "firm but fair" enforcement of a program of corrective or progressive discipline. The habitual absentee should be warned, counseled, reprimanded, suspended, and eventually discharged if the problem is not corrected.

• Reduction of absenteeism through group incentives. Peer pressure is an effective means for making the behavior of individuals conform to the collective will of the group. The education of employees concerning the costs of absenteeism coupled with a mechanism for distributing the savings realized from reduced absences are necessary steps toward focusing group pressure upon the chronic absentee to develop better work habits. Employees, cognizant of the monetary rewards stemming from reduced absenteeism, have an incentive to "persuade" problem workers to adjust their behavior to conform to the wishes of the group.

The profit-sharing provisions of the new General Motors–United Automobile Workers contract provide an excellent opportunity for implementing collective incentives to reduce absenteeism.[16] Employees with good attendance records could be issued General Motors stock in an amount equal to 35 percent of the cost savings resulting from reduced worker absences. This percentage represents the proportion of total production costs due to worker compensation and is generally accepted as an equitable method for distributing productivity gains. Assuming that peer pressure leads to a reduction in the absenteeism from 5 percent to .83 percent (as discussed earlier), the work force would be entitled to 35 percent of the resulting savings of $834 million—or $292 million in General Motors stock. Given a labor force of 479,000 employees, each worker would receive $610 in General Motors stock.

For some bargaining relationships, particularly those characterized by labor-management conflict, the group incentive approach represents a more workable alternative to reducing absences than the other methods noted above. Where mature bargaining relationships exist, labor and management may want to combine the group incentive approach with the first two methods.

SUMMARY

Casual absences represent rational employee response to contractually structured or administered incentives to stay away from the job. The chronic absentee, whose tastes reflect a greater preference for leisure than that of the majority of workers, reacts by choosing additional leisure. Although unauthorized by the contract, additional leisure is, nevertheless, one of the options available under the contract. The effective hourly wage–fringe benefit structure creates the incentive to take leisure, while employer acceptance of absenteeism through non-enforcement of discipline enables employees to capitalize upon that incentive. The fact that 85 percent of all casual absences are attributable to 10 percent of the work force supports this observation.

Absenteeism is due to poorly worded and administered contract provisions which permit employees to obtain windfall gains through unauthorized time off.

The responsibility for a serviceable contract rests with management and labor. In addition to clearly reflecting the needs and desires of both parties at the time of contract negotiations, the provisions should be firmly and fairly enforced during the life of the contract. Just as good work habits reflect the foresight and hard work of labor and management in contract negotiation and administration, excessive absenteeism indicates a job poorly done. Management and labor have no one to blame but themselves for excessive absences due to inappropriate language and nonenforcement of discipline. Correction of the absenteeism problem will require a high degree of cooperation between General Motors and the United Automobile Workers as well as a strong commitment to eliminate contract-based and administered causes of casual absences.

As subsequently occurred and as described in Chapter 5, General Motors and the United Auto Workers have cooperated and made a strong commitment to eliminate casual absences. The impact of their effort is discussed in Chapter 10.

NOTES

1. "Agreement between General Motors Corporation and the UAW," November 22, 1976 (effective December 13, 1976); renegotiated September 14, 1979 (effective October 1, 1979).

2. General Motors Corporation Personnel Administration and Development Staff Report, "Absenteeism and General Motors: A Step Toward Understanding" (January 1979):40–3; Richard O'Brian, director of compensation for General Motors Corporation, reaffirmed the results of this study by telephone in November 1979.

3. All data used in this paper were provided by Richard O'Brian, director of compensation for General Motors Corporation, unless otherwise stated. Compensation figures refer to the 1976–1979 contract.

4. Calculated: 5% × 500,000 employees = 25,000 employees.

5. Calculated: $20 × 50 million man hours = $1 billion.

6. United States Department of Health, Education, and Welfare, Public Health Service, National Center for Health Statistics, Current Estimates from the Health Interview Survey: United States—1977 (Hyattsville, Md.; DHEW Publication No. (PHS) 78–1554, September 1978), p. 18.

7. Employer costs associated with absenteeism are discussed in United States Department of Labor, Manpower Administration, Suggestions for Control of Turnover and Absenteeism (Washington, D.C.: U.S. Government Printing Office, 1972).

8. Calculated: 25,000 workers × hours × $5 fringe benefits × 250 scheduled work days = $250 million.

9. Calculated: 25,000 workers × 8 hours × $15 wage/fringe benefit rate × 250 scheduled work days = $750 million.

10. Calculated: 20,850 workers × 8 hours × $5 fringe benefits × 250 scheduled work days = $209 million. Calculated: $209 million + [20,850 workers × 8 hours × $15 wage/fringe benefit rate × 250 scheduled work days] = $209 million + $625 million = $834 million.

11. Marcia L. Greenbaum, "The Shorter Workweek," in E. Wright Bakke, Clark Kerr, and Charles W. Anrod (eds.), Unions, Management and the Public (New York: Harcourt, Brace, 1967), p. 435.

12. See the following: L. W. Porter and R. M. Steers, "Organizational Work and Personal Factors in Employee Turnover and Absenteeism," *Psychological Bulletin* (1973):151–165; J. N. Hedges, "Absence from Work—A Look at Some Data," *Monthly Labor Review* (1973):24–30; "Employee Absenteeism and Turnover," in *Personnel Policies Forum* (Washington, D.C.: Bureau of National Affairs, 1974); J. F. Baum and S. A. Youngblood, "Impact of an Organizational Control Policy on Absenteeism, Performance, and Satisfaction," *Journal of Applied Psychology* (1975):688–694; N. Nicholson, "Management Sanctions and Absence Control," *Human Relations* (1976): 139–150; John F. Baum, "Effectiveness of an Attendance Control Policy in Reducing Chronic Absenteeism," *Personnel Psychology* (Spring 1978), 31:71–81.

13. Although the figure portrays the case of a typical absentee, the factors responsible for the absentee's behavior are operational in the case of workers with good work habits—but to a lesser extent.

14. In terms of the figure, the average effective hourly wage rate for a specific number of hours worked is represented by the slope of a straight line drawn from point O to the point on the earnings line which corresponds to the specified number of hours worked. As is apparent, the slopes of these lines (that is, OA, OB, OC, OD, OE, and OF) decline as the number of hours worked increases.

15. "Lessons from Japan, Inc.," *Newsweek* (September 8, 1980):61–62. "One Dark Cloud over Aerospace," *Business Week* (September 29, 1980):110–112.

16. "Agreement between General Motors Corporation and the UAW."

7 Effective Grievance Management: A Complement to Absenteeism Control

Man's capacity for justice makes democracy possible, but man's inclination to injustice makes democracy necessary.

Reinhold Niebuhr
The Children of Light and the Children of Darkness

There is no grievance that is a fit object of redress by mob law.

Abraham Lincoln
Address at the Young Men's Lyceum
Springfield, Illinois, January 17, 1838

Recompense injury with justice, and recompense kindness with kindness.

Confucius
The Confucian Analects

Worker alienation frequently manifests itself through the filing of formal grievances instead of absenteeism. In either case, the firm suffers. This chapter examines grievances in detail—their cause, settlement, and prevention. Since grievances and absences are alternate forms in which worker alienation may manifest itself (two sides of the same coin, so to speak) the prevention of grievances through the elimination of their underlying causes (that is, worker alienation and frustration in various forms) is also an effective method for controlling absenteeism. Hence, this chapter completes the formulation and explanation of a comprehensive, integrated program for absenteeism control begun in Chapter 5. In short, one cannot talk about the prevention of absenteeism without also talking about grievance minimization and prevention. The two topics are inextricably intertwined.

The following material is applicable to both union and nonunion firms. Grievances are endemic to the employer-employee relationship and are not a

The material contained herein was first published as: Clarence R. Deitsch and David A. Dilts, "Effective Grievance Management: Holding Grievances Down," *Prentice-Hall Industrial Relations Guide Service* (January 29, 1980) 21:42,277–42,288B. Reprinted by permission.

greater problem for organized businesses than nonorganized businesses. Indeed, a large number of unresolved grievances oftentimes prompts employees to look outside the organization (that is, to unionization) for remedies to what are perceived to be unsatisfactory work conditions and dysfunctional channels of communication.

THE GRIEVANCE PROCEDURE

The grievance procedure stands as the cornerstone of the industrial system of jurisprudence. This mechanism performs the same function for contract law that the multitiered judicial system performs for the body of federal, state, and local law. The multitiered grievance structure is the vehicle through which the private law of the collective bargaining agreement is interpreted and given meaning as the contract is applied and administered by management in the day-to-day operation of the firm.[1] Further, just as the judicial structure provides due process for the protection of the rights of the general citizenry, the grievance structure provides due process for the protection of the contractual rights of employees.

The specific form that the grievance procedure takes will vary from one employment relationship to the next, depending upon the individual needs, personalities, characteristics, and circumstances of each relationship. In short, there is not one structural form for the grievance procedure that is appropriate for every employment relationship. Labor and management should adopt the structure that best facilitates the prompt and impartial adjudication of grievances. The equitable resolution of grievances through an appropriately structured, widely understood, and efficiently functioning grievance mechanism is the first step toward meeting basic employee needs for security, recognition, participation, and control of those forces that influence their lives; it is an absolute prerequisite for effective grievance management. Delays in grievance resolution caused by poorly designed grievance structures create frustration, insecurity, and mistrust, thereby generating additional grievances that eventually burden and overtax the grievance procedure.

PHILOSOPHY OF CONTRACT ADMINISTRATION

Grievances are costly to both management and labor. Every grievance diverts resources away from the operation of the firm to the dispute settlement process. In addition to these obvious costs, there are long-run costs resulting from the harmful impact that grievances have upon the labor-management relationship. At best, grievance adjudication is a "negative sum game." The "winner" of the dispute simply regains whatever it was that was threatened or lost as a result of the other party's action; there is not a net gain. "Victory" neither removes the antagonism generated by the grievance and the resulting harm done the relationship nor does it recover the resources expended by the disputants during grievance adjudication.

As substantial as the costs of grievance adjudication are, these costs are insignificant in comparison to the benefits produced by an efficiently functioning grievance procedure. Further, these costs can be reduced by management adoption of an appropriate philosophy of contract administration. In those labor-management relationships where the grievance procedure has become overtaxed (that is, where the costs of grievance adjudication are unacceptably high), this state of affairs can, in a large percentage of the cases, be traced to the advocate-conflict philosophy of contract administration.

The grievance procedure is only as effective as the philosophy of contract administration that guides its use. The traditional action-reaction philosophy of contract administration by nature breeds mistrust and hostility, thereby generating unnecessary and avoidable grievances. Effective grievance management mandates a philosophy of contract administration that not only views the grievance procedure as the most important communications vehicle of the labor-management relationship, but also accepts the systematic elimination of the underlying causes of grievances as the basis for grievance minimization. Once adopted, the "developing communication" philosophy of contract administration facilitates, indeed, it necessitates, the implementation of various techniques to reduce the number of grievances.

CAUSES OF GRIEVANCES

Grievances are, at the same time, both similar and dissimilar. Although unique in terms of personnel, human needs, contractual provisions, past practice (shop common law), economic conditions, and other factors involved, every grievance is rational from some perspective; self-interest, however perceived, is served or promoted by the filing of the grievance. Notwithstanding their diversity, grievances can be classified into three categories by cause and type of self-interest served: grievances caused by misunderstanding; grievances caused by intentional contract violations; and grievances that are symptomatic of problems outside the scope of the labor agreement.

Misunderstanding

Misunderstanding encompasses grievances filed as a result of either disputed facts surrounding the application of specific contractual provisions, disagreements concerning the proper interpretation of contract provisions, or a general lack of familiarity with the labor agreement. Whatever the source of misunderstanding, self-interest motivates the aggrieved party to utilize the grievance procedure in an attempt to protect contractual rights or what are perceived to be contractual rights.

Grievances stemming from disputed facts in the administration of specific contract provisions are, for the most part, inevitable even in the most mature and efficient of bargaining relationships. For example, there will always be disputes concerning the guilt or innocence of employees who are disciplined for alleged violations of the labor agreement, not to mention the reasonableness or fairness of the discipline imposed. The American system of jurisprudence, after which the industrial system of jurisprudence is modeled, assumes an individual to be innocent until proven guilty. Hence, grievances concerning the facts of a case are to be expected in the day-to-day administration of the contract. Indeed, the fact that such grievances are filed indicates that the parties to collective bargaining perceive the grievance procedure as guaranteeing due process for the protection of contractual rights—a prerequisite for an efficiently functioning grievance procedure.

An ambiguous contract is a constant source of grievances. Language that is clear and unequivocal to many individuals may not convey the same meaning to others. Although explicit contract language significantly reduces possible areas of misunderstanding, it will not make the meaning of agreed-to contract terms intuitively obvious in all cases. On the other hand, bargaining relationships characterized by an unusually large number of grievances due to contract ambiguity indicate that labor and management have inadequately discharged their collective bargaining responsibilities during contract negotiations. For example, the intent of a contract clause requiring the promotion of the "senior qualified" person to a better paying position could have been clarified by posing the following questions at the time the provision was agreed to: Which is the key word for purposes of promotion, "senior" or "qualified"? How are qualifications to be determined? On what basis is seniority measured? Similar questions concerning all contract provisions, raised and resolved during the negotiation process, will minimize grievances during the life of the contract. An effectively functioning grievance procedure demands foresight and hard work during contract negotiations.

Regardless of how well the contract is written and understood by the negotiating parties, grievances will still arise if the document goes unread by those persons who are charged with, or affected by, its application and enforcement. Whether the cause is ignorance of the contract on the part of the first-line supervisor, the union steward, or the employees, the end product is the same: needless and avoidable grievances.

Although contract ignorance, wherever found, is inexcusable, it is somewhat more understandable in the case of first-line supervisors. Supervisors typically are not rewarded for effective grievance management. Rather, rewards are normally tied to the achievement of production goals. The link between effective grievance management and the achievement of production goals is either overlooked or not well understood. Hence, the contract is frequently ignored.

While somewhat more understandable, the myopic production-motivated behavior of supervisors is at the same time potentially more harmful to the labor-management relationship than employee ignorance of the same contract. The ineptitude of supervisors in contract administration spawns aggressive employee behavior. Subjected to the pressure of meeting production targets and simultaneously besieged by employee grievances, supervisors again resort to expediency by accommodating employee demands in whatever fashion necessary to maintain production, thereby providing further incentives for the filing of grievances. The result is a body of precedents that undermines the contract.

Intentional Contract Violations

Grievances falling within this category are either the result of a cognizant disregard of contract provisions or efforts to capitalize upon ambiguous contract language and past practice. Since management is responsible for active contract administration, it has a greater number of opportunities for deliberate contract infractions than does labor. The temptation to violate the contract occasionally becomes irresistible. These violations are usually rationalized on the grounds of being economically imperative or of little substantive importance to employees. On the other hand, contract ambiguities in conjunction with favorably perceived past practice, "aided and abetted" by a management policy of "caving in" to union claims, provide incentives to employees to file grievances. The employees hope to gain through the grievance and arbitration process what they were unable to achieve at the bargaining table. In each of the above cases, grievances arise because the parties, in pursuit of self-interest, attempt to achieve some right or privilege not explicitly conveyed by the contract.

Symptomatic Grievances

Symptomatic grievances constitute the final category of grievances. These grievances are the most troublesome in terms of diagnosis and prevention. As the name implies, the grievance itself is not the underlying problem, but simply the vehicle through which the employee registers disillusionment and frustration with either job or non–job-related problems. The causes of symptomatic grievances are many: personal problems (for example, drinking), marital difficulties, union politics, unfavorable contract language, or the basic inabilities to achieve self-actualization (that is, the need to achieve self-fulfillment and realization of potential). The case of the disgruntled cook immediately comes to mind. When the newly hired cook worked with the person she was to replace, her work and disposition were both exceptionally good. When she was required to perform the same duties on her own, her work and attitude deteriorated, and she began filing grievances. Quite by accident while in conversation with her, the industrial relations manager discovered the problem: the cook could not read. Consequently, when the previous cook, upon whom she depended for verbal directions (cues) departed, the cook could not read recipes, that is, execute her job responsibilities, thus creating frustration and generating the filing of trivial grievances. Given the basic need of employees to vent frustration and the fact that the problems referred to above do not constitute grounds for legitimate grievances, employees resort to filing trivial complaints. In short, the filing of

trivial grievances is in the employees' self-interest; these symptomatic grievances are a form of compensation, even if only a channel for venting frustration, for personal failures and inadequacies in other areas.

Two types of symptomatic grievances warrant further consideration as well
as a word of caution for those charged with contract administration. First,
grievances generated by internal union politics represent a "no win" situation
for managers. Special efforts to resolve grievances presented by one political
faction of the union precipitate grievances in protest on the part of other political factions. Management, in spite of its good intentions, will inevitably find
itself embroiled in internal union affairs. The only course of action open to
management in this environment is strict neutrality.

Second, a symptomatic grievance designed to highlight unfavorable contract
provisions should be recognized for what it is: a bargaining tactic to bring about
change in contract provisions. Historical studies of the frequency of grievance
filing indicate that the number of grievances filed increases as contract expira-
tion dates draw near. "Overloading the grievance procedure" has long been
recognized as a favorite bargaining tactic of unions. As such, symptomatic
grievances of this nature are best handled at the negotiating table and not during
the administration of the soon-to-expire contract.

GRIEVANCE MINIMIZATION TECHNIQUES

The following suggested methods for holding down grievances may not be
appropriate in every labor-management relationship. The feasibility of implementing various techniques will depend upon, for example, the maturity of the
bargaining relationship, that is, whether the relationship is characterized by conflict
or whether it is characterized by cooperation. Cooperation is typically the product of several years of interaction between the bargaining parties; it is an un-
realistic expectation in newly established relationships that are often the result
of long and bitter union organizational drives. Thus, the methods suggested
constitute an arsenal of techniques to be selectively utilized as bargaining circumstances and the underlying causes of grievances dictate.

Table Bargaining

An efficiently functioning grievance and arbitration procedure reflects the
wisdom, foresight, and hard work of labor and management during contract negotiations. There is no single more important technique for preventing grievances than the negotiation of clear and unequivocal contract language. Any and
all questions that the contracting parties have in their own minds concerning
the phrasing, wording, and meaning of specific clauses should be raised and
resolved at the time of the table bargaining sessions. If separate "articles of
understanding" are necessary to pinpoint the meaning of contract provisions,
labor and management are wise to put forth the extra effort required to write

such addenda to the agreement. Otherwise, grievances will invariably arise in these same areas during contract administration.

A serviceable contract provision not only requires clarity of meaning but also must meet the needs of the contracting parties. A sure way to generate grievances is for labor and management to adopt language simply because that language has been successful elsewhere. Each bargaining relationship is unique; language that has served one relationship well will not necessarily be functional for another. Hence, contractual provisions should be tailored to meet the specific and disparate needs of each labor-management relationship.

Contract Proselytization

Does a falling tree make a sound if there is no one in the forest to hear it? Everyone has at one time been asked this question. The question, modified and applied to labor-management relations, highlights one of the major obstacles to effective grievance management. Does a serviceable collective bargaining agreement, the provisions of which are incontrovertible as to meaning, reduce the number of grievances if the contract is not read and understood by those responsible for administering the document? While the answer to the tree question is still argued in some quarters, the answer to the contract question is an unchallenged "no."

Effective grievance management demands that management and union personnel at all levels be well educated as to the letter and intent of each contract clause. A particularly effective method of familiarizing supervisory personnel and union representatives with the contract is through the use of joint training sessions, with labor-management negotiators acting as training session group leaders. As the contract is read from beginning to end, supervisors and union representatives should be given the opportunity to raise substantive questions concerning the meaning of each contract provision. When questions concerning meaning do arise, these may be resolved in consensus fashion prior to moving on to subsequent provisions. A second round of meetings between union representatives and rank-and-file members is then required to convey to employees the consensus meaning of the labor-management joint training sessions. In short, the training sessions and meetings are intended to weed out misunderstanding as a potential cause of grievances as far as is possible.

Joint training sessions also reduce grievances in three other important ways. First, negotiators, cognizant of the fact that the product of their bargaining efforts will be closely scrutinized and that they will be questioned concerning the meaning of various contract provisions by those groups that they represent, will have a greater incentive to tailor, in unequivocal terms, the contract to fit the needs of the bargaining relationship. Second, the sessions give upper echelon management the opportunity to interact with first-line supervisors. Effective contract administration should be stressed in these meetings as the critical factor for the achievement of individual production goals. Since rewards are normally tied to the achievement of production goals, first-line supervisors will develop a greater commitment to effective contract administration. Finally, joint training sessions promote an atmosphere of cooperation and conciliation that are characteristic of mature bargaining relationships wherein intentional contract violations and, therefore, resulting grievances are small in number.

Contract Administration

Although effective table bargaining in conjunction with sustained efforts to familiarize all parties concerned with the meaning of contract provisions will eliminate many of the causes of grievances, these techniques need to be supplemented by a philosophy of contract administration that eliminates the incentives to file grievances.

The "developing communication" philosophy of contract administration discussed earlier reduces misunderstanding as a basic cause of grievances and eliminates incentives to file grievances as well. Indeed, joint training sessions are but the first important aspect of this philosophy. The training sessions demonstrate management concern for the protection of employee contractual rights. If successful, there will be fewer management contract infractions that lead to grievances, and, as a result of the atmosphere of trust and cooperation created by the training sessions, there will be less of a propensity on the part of employees to perceive and file grievances.

The second important component of the developing communication philosophy of contract administration (that is, the component responsible for reduced incentives to file grievances) is the "firm but fair" approach to grievance adjudication. Employees often become aggressive in filing grievances simply because they have discovered over time that aggressive behavior yields results. Self-interest motivates employees to take advantage of any opportunity to achieve rights and privileges not specified by the contract.

The grievance procedure, not to mention the contract, is undermined whenever management takes a reasonable position on the disputed issue but yields in the face of actual or threatened economic pressure. The firm but fair approach to grievance adjudication requires management to investigate fully all relevant facts, to analyze carefully applicable contract provisions, to develop a reasonable position on the basis of the information at its disposal, and to adhere firmly to said position when challenged. Adoption of this approach does not mean that management will not listen to opposing arguments, cannot be swayed by convincing evidence, will not change its position if proven to be incorrect, or will not renegotiate weak or inoperative contract provisions. The firm but fair policy, however, does mean that management will not yield to actual or threatened pressure. The above policy reduces grievances, whereas a policy of appeasement encourages grievances.

The developing communication philosophy of contract administration is incompatible with a management policy of permitting the development of past practices that contravene the language and spirit of the labor agreement. Such a body of past practices serves only to increase the incentives for employees to file grievances. On the other hand, past practice that is mutual in nature and that clarifies ambiguous contract language reinforces the recommended philosophy of contract administration by strengthening cooperation. However, labor and management are wise to incorporate in or append to the contract a statement detailing the role past practice is to play in the bargaining relationship.

Human Relations

Although a well-structured grievance procedure, underpinned and guided by the developing communication philosophy of contract administration, meets basic employee needs for security, participation, and recognition, thereby eliminating some of the causes of symptomatic grievances, it cannot, nor should it attempt to, eradicate the frustration associated with the personal inadequacies and failures of each employee in job- and non–job-related areas. In attempting to do everything for every employee, the likelihood is that the grievance procedure would become overtaxed and less than effective in all areas. What is required is an adjunct to the grievance procedure and philosophy of contract administration that can attend to and reduce the causes of symptomatic grievances.

In the wake of growing worker alienation in recent years, many firms have established human relations departments to handle employee problems and complaints regardless of origin. The express mission of these departments has been the reduction of symptomatic grievances through the resolution of personal problems which lead either to job-related problems (for example, drunkenness) culminating in disciplinary actions and accompanying grievances or to the filing of trivial grievances due to frustration. Since human relations departments have been structured to operate more or less independently of the industrial relations departments of most firms, employees do not perceive the departments as posing a threat through contract administration and enforcement. Typical services and solutions to problems have included general employee counseling, referral of employees to private and community organizations for specialized counseling, removal of or additional training for first-line supervisors insensitive to employee needs, promotion of previously overqualified personnel, additional training and schooling of underqualified employees at company expense, and the establishment of a system of rewards for cost-minimizing suggestions. Similar departments might prove worthwhile for other firms where grievance procedures have become burdened by symptomatic grievances.

SUMMARY

Successful utilization of the various techniques of grievance minimization described in this chapter necessitates the establishment of an appropriately structured, widely understood, and efficiently functioning grievance structure and the adoption of a clinical rather than a legalistic philosophy of contract administration. The clinical philosophy of contract administration views the grievance procedure as the most important communications vehicle of the labor-management relationship and accepts grievance minimization through a systematic elimination of the underlying causes as the *raison d'être* of contract administration.

Implementation of the steps necessary to bring about a reduction in grievances also requires an atmosphere of trust and cooperation. Honesty and credibility are absolute prerequisites for the development of this atmosphere. Dishonesty, more than any other factor, can destroy progress toward grievance minimization. It undermines cooperation, thereby scuttling the possibility of collective problem solving.

Grievances will always occur, but they need not be numerous, burden the grievance procedure, nor weaken the bargaining relationship if approached with honesty and a spirit of cooperation. In short, effective grievance management requires a strong joint labor-management commitment to eliminate the underlying causes of grievances.

NOTES

1. In those cases where a formal collective bargaining agreement does not exist (that is, nonunion firms), management-determined personnel policies and rules constitute the equivalent of private contract law.

8 Absenteeism Policy and Its Administration: An Arbitrator's View

The company had the right to unilaterally establish the absentee control program. Nothing in the contract prevented it. The contract impliedly as well as expressly reserved certain rights to management. The right to develop internal procedures and records systems would seem to be among such impliedly reserved management rights. Developing standard operating procedures for managerial personnel to follow also would appear to be a prerogative impliedly reserved to management. . . .

I conclude that the Company's unilateral establishment of the absentee control program was not prohibited by the contract, and that it was a proper exercise of a reserved management right to manage the plant efficiently.

Arbitrator John A. Bailey
64 LA 1288, 1288

If the just cause standard is to have any real meaning in contract administration, Management cannot abdicate its responsibility to undertake the onerous task of distinguishing between wrongful conduct meriting discipline and unfortunate circumstances, which despite production exigencies, demand a limited forebearance. . . .

Failure to distinguish between legitimate excuses for absence and reprehensible misconduct is repugnant to fundamental notions of fair play whenever it results in an employee whose absence is for legitimate reason beyond his control being treated as harshly as a deliberate wrongdoer.

Arbitrator James C. Duff
593 F.2d 316, 317, n.4, 100 LRRM 2846.

THE TENSION BETWEEN MANAGEMENT RIGHTS AND JUST CAUSE: TWO VIEWS OF JUST CAUSE

The foregoing passages represent two different perspectives regarding limits on management's right to manage and typify what Fairweather characterized as the

"Tension between Management Rights and Just Cause."[1] On one hand, there are those who see management's right to discipline limited only by considerations of what is necessary to maintain efficient organizational operation. Here, operational efficiency sanctions managerial discipline and constitutes just cause for discipline. Just cause exists whenever an affirmative answer can be given to the question, "Does the disciplinary action sustain operational efficiency?" Accordingly, management would have the right to establish and enforce a dress code for employees while at work but not away from work, the presumption being that such a code promotes organizational productivity in the first case but serves no functional purpose in the second. For those taking this position, a contract clause requiring just cause for discipline simply reaffirms rather than restricts management's right to direct the work force, set hours, and make rules—the right to manage. Such a clause is not viewed as a limit.

Where management residual rights advocates stress managerial responsibility and accountability and the concomitant need for the freedom to discharge its obligations to stockholders, others would emphasize that management has a broader responsibility, to employees as well as to stockholders. As a result, the functional view of just cause must be adjusted accordingly. For these individuals, a contractual requirement of just cause for discipline must be viewed more in the nature of a true limitation upon management's right to direct and discipline the work force. Specifically, discipline undertaken to accomplish functional organizational objectives must be assessed in a reasonable, evenhanded, and nondiscriminatory fashion in accordance with corrective and progressive principles of discipline. In short, management's responsibility to its employees superimposes fairness and corrective discipline standards upon the functional test standard for purposes of determining whether just cause for discipline existed. Each of these standards and its relationship to the functional test standard is examined below.

The Fairness Standard

Misconceptions abound concerning the requirement that discipline be administered in an objective, dispassionate and evenhanded fashion—in short, concerning the fairness standard. The most common misconception is that the standard requires management to assess the same penalty for the same rule infraction—that different penalties for the same rule infraction constitute, per se, proof that management's action was disparate, discriminatory, unduly severe, or otherwise arbitrary. Quite the contrary, the standard anticipates a spectrum of possible penalties, the severity of which fits the severity of the specific rule infraction as judged by management in light of all relevant circumstances, the latter being defined to include the nature of the offense, the degree of fault, tenure of employment, personnel record, degree of provocation, and other mitigating or extenuating circumstances. To establish discrimination, it must be shown that there was unlike treatment in like circumstances, not unlike treatment in unlike circumstances. Where circumstances vary, different penalties are permitted.

Broadly and positively speaking, the fairness standard requires management to proceed cautiously and prudently, to conduct an unbiased and unemotional investigation, to weigh the facts carefully in light of relevant circumstances, and to assess ultimately a penalty commensurate with the severity of the rule infraction determined against the backdrop of said circumstances. Probably the best statement or explanation of the limitations (or lack thereof) placed upon management's right to direct and discipline the work force toward achievement of organizational objectives (that is, the functional test standard) by the fairness standard is that of Arbitrator Whitley P. McCoy in *Stockham Pipe Fittings Co.*[2]

Where an employee has violated a rule or engaged in conduct meriting disciplinary action, it is primarily the function of management to decide upon the proper penalty. If management acts in good faith upon a fair investigation and fixes a penalty not inconsistent with that imposed in other like cases, an arbitrator should not disturb it. The mere fact that management has imposed a somewhat different penalty or a somewhat more severe penalty than the arbitrator would have, if he had had the decision to make originally, is no justification for changing it. The minds of equally reasonable men differ. A consideration which would weigh heavily with one man will seem of less importance to another. A circumstance which highly aggravates an offense in one man's eyes may be only slight aggravation to another. If an arbitrator could substitute his judgment and discretion for the judgment and discretion honestly exercised by management, then the functions of management would have been abdicated, and unions would take every case to arbitration. The result would be as intolerable to employees as to management. The only circumstances under which a penalty imposed by management can be rightfully set aside by an arbitrator are those where discrimination, unfairness, or capricious and arbitrary action are proved—in other words, where there has been abuse of discretion.

Corrective-Progressive Discipline

The purpose of discipline is behavior modification: the modification of an individual's on-the-job behavior in order that the organization's goals and objectives might be achieved. Given its inherent purpose, job-related discipline must be reasonable and fair; the severity of the penalty must match the severity of the infraction, must be appropriate to the offense. Penalties that are too severe, for example, create a morale problem that may surface in the form of an unacceptably high turnover rate, to name but one of a number of possible counterproductive employee responses. On the other hand, penalties that are too light add insult to injury. Not only do they fail to channel employee actions in the desired direction, but they spawn employee contempt as well. In short, the desired changes in employee behavior will not occur unless penalties are appropriate for the infractions. The overriding concern of industrial-commercial discipline, therefore, should be its corrective impact. Punitive discipline, punishment for the sake of punishment, has no productive role to play in the modern labor management relationship. Corrective discipline, on the other hand, is intended to modify behavior and is indispensable to good management.

Each employee normally represents a significant investment in human capital on the part of the employer, not to mention the search and screening costs to hire the employee in the first instance. For most employees and types of infractions, corrective discipline is less costly than exclusion. It precludes the necessity of recapitalization; it is the least costly alternative open to the employer.

Habitual and Incidental Offenses: When and Where to Use Corrective Discipline

The nature of the infraction to a large extent dictates the procedure to be followed in the assessment of discipline—whether a definite progression of steps (for example, oral warning, written warning, suspension, and termination) should be followed and the severity of the penalties therein. Normally, the more serious the offense, the fewer the sequential steps that are required. Certain types of conduct are better candidates for formalized corrective discipline than others. Particularly appropriate infractions are those that reoccur in some pattern. These habitual offenses include tardiness, absenteeism, drunkenness, poor workmanship, and failure to make production rates. On the other hand, incidental offenses, which include crimes against society (for example, theft, assault, battery, rape) as well as certain violations of shop rules may not warrant progression from a less to a more severe penalty, as noted by Fairweather:

> Certain types of conduct are beyond the correction limits. An employee discharged for stealing from a fellow employee's locker should not be reinstated on the premise that his or her "light finger" techniques will disappear, many employers believe. No employee has one "free steal"—a theft without discharge.[3]

Employee negligence that threatens the health and safety of other employees or an employer's productive property also falls into this category. An employer must have the ability to protect property and life by terminating the negligent employee at the time the disputed behavior first occurs. In still other cases, the employee can be viewed as discharging himself or herself—having had and passed up the opportunity to apply his or her own corrective discipline. The clearest example of self-discharge is the case where an employee, having been clearly warned that his or her continued refusal to follow instructions will result in termination, nevertheless persists in such a refusal. Here, failure to follow instructions becomes insubordination, with termination the appropriate penalty; the employee failed to heed the warning by taking appropriate corrective action and, therefore, discharged himself or herself.

When formal progressive discipline is called for, contracts typically take one of two possible approaches. They may spell out, step by step, the progression required from less to more severe penalties, or they may leave the appropriate progression to managerial discretion. Contract provisions such as "violation of shop disciplinary and safety rules may lead to discipline up to and including discharge" are characteristic of the latter approach to progressive discipline. Under this approach, a probationary period after which an employee's disciplinary slate will be wiped clean (that is, a kind of "statute of limitations") as well as the assessment of penalties that are less severe than would appear to be warranted by the severity of the offense are matters of managerial leniency. On the other hand, when progression from a less severe to a more severe penalty is contractually specified and mandated, the statute of limitations issue is handled by means of an amnesty provision. This is a contract clause that specifies that an employee's personnel record will be cleansed of any discipline provided the employee does not violate shop disciplinary and safety rules for some specified period of time.

ABSENTEEISM CONTROL: THE EPITOME OF MANAGERIAL FRUSTRATION

Nowhere is the tension between managerial prerogative and just cause—between the functional test, fairness, and corrective discipline standards for purposes of determining the existence of just cause—greater than in the area of employee maintenance of a regular work schedule. Indeed, probably the single most difficult area of contract administration and enforcement involves the assessment of discipline for excessive absence, the latter broadly defined to include tardiness, a form of absenteeism which many managers consider more bothersome than total absence of work. The inherent difficulty of the problem can be gauged from the fact that the vast majority of arbitrators cringe upon being notified of their selection to adjudicate an absenteeism-related discipline dispute; most would gladly trade one such case for a half dozen of the more traditional contract interpretation disputes. This instinctive reluctance to hear absenteeism cases can be traced to two factors: the unpleasant nature of any type of discipline and the so-called gray areas that appear to be legion in absenteeism-related disputes. While little can be done to eliminate entirely the unpleasant nature of discipline, it can be made more palatable by bringing certain issues and criteria into sharper focus, by reducing the so-called gray areas surrounding the assessment of discipline for excessive absenteeism. The following paragraphs constitute just such an attempt.

Culpable and Nonculpable Absences

Managers readily excuse occasional absences due to illness. Managers, however, have the right and the duty to protect their institutions from the harmful effects of excessive absenteeism, whatever its cause. Given the need of an enterprise to efficiently accomplish its objectives, discipline up to and including termination of employees who deliberately or carelessly fail to execute their end of the employment contract—that is, maintain a regular, productive work schedule—is understandable, reasonable, and justifiable. Likewise, termination of employees whose poor health precludes regular work attendance is understandable, reasonable, and justifiable.

Suspending such an employee makes no sense; if punishment would cure legitimate physical disability, there would be no need for medical doctors. An employer has no power to discipline employees for conduct that is not culpable in any sense. Furthermore, it is manifestly counterproductive to force a genuinely ill employee to miss additional work, by suspending him or her, as a measure intended to improve attendance.[4]

Here, where absences do not involve culpability, fairness dictates a greater degree of forebearance than where absences do involve culpability, namely, the waiver of intermediate disciplinary steps until such time that nonculpable absences become unreasonable and justify termination. In both cases, absences that involve culpability and those that do not, arbitrators recognize the right and responsibility of management to discipline or terminate, as circumstances warrant, when absences become excessive in nature. Arbitrators, however, do require managers to differentiate between the two in whatever system they devise to track and control chronic absenteeism. Take away said differentiation and just cause evaporates.

The Need for a Well-Structured, Unequivocal, and Understandable Statement of Shop Rules, Attendant Penalties, and Corrective-Progressive Discipline

Despite arbitral recognition of management's right to discipline for excessive absences, supervisors have been regularly frustrated in the practical application of this right; arbitrators have set aside discipline for excessive absenteeism in a large percentage of cases. Rather than reflecting a built-in bias for unions or callousness toward organizational goals, these decisions are oftentimes prompted by what arbitrators perceive to be violations of the most fundamental employer responsibility to employees, namely, the development of unequivocal and understandable rules and regulations. In other words, the arbitrator balances the supervisor's right to discipline against the employee's right to know what is expected of him or her. Professors Slichter, Healy, and Livernash cite the following language as an example of a well-structured, unequivocal, and understandable statement of shop rules, attendant penalties, and use of corrective and progressive discipline:

In a Plant community such as ours, there are certain regulations which govern the conduct of employees on Company property, just as there are regulations covering citizens in the community in which you live. These regulations—which are an aid to maintaining safe and desirable working conditions for everyone—are posted for general information and to assure uniform administration of disciplinary action if ever it is necessary. These regulations are divided into three main groups, depending upon the disciplinary action which must be taken. For violation of any plant rule, a written report must be completed promptly by employee's supervisor.

A. A violation of any of the following regulations by an employee is considered inexcusable and will result in immediate discharge:
1. Deliberate damage to Company property or to the property of other employees.
2. Stealing.
3. Fighting.
4. Carrying concealed weapons or any other violation of criminal laws.
5. Immoral conduct or indecency.
6. Willful hampering of production or failure to carry out definite instructions or assignments.
7. Gross insubordination.
8. Falsification of records.
9. Hiding, concealing or the misappropriation of Company property or the property of other employees.
10. Gambling or conducting gambling activities.
11. Sleeping on the job.
12. Punching clock card of another employee.
B. The violation of any of the following rules by an employee is considered a serious misconduct. The first violation of any of these rules will be punishable by three days off without pay. The second violation of any of these regulations will result in release.
1. Careless waste of materials or abuse of tools and equipment.
2. Possessing intoxicants or drugs in the plant or reporting to work under the influence of intoxicants or drugs.
3. Insubordination.
4. Playing of pranks or "horseplay."
5. Unauthorized selling, soliciting or canvassing.
6. Disorderly conduct.
7. Producing or concealing defective work through obvious carelessness or negligence.
8. Abusive or threatening language.
9. Excessive absence from work or habitual tardiness.
C. The violation of any of the following regulations by an employee is considered misconduct and is not to be tolerated. The first offense will bring a reprimand. The second offense will be punishable by three days off without pay. Any further offense may result in release.
1. Absence from work area without permission or satisfactory excuse.
2. Loitering.
3. Leaving job or work area before end of shift.
4. Failure to report personal injury.
5. Smoking in prohibited areas.
6. Posting unauthorized notices, defacing walls, or tampering with bulletin boards.
7. Wage attachments.

8. Improper parking or improper operation of cars on Company property.
9. Unreported absence or absence without justifiable cause.[5]

Even here, however, as is all too common in absenteeism-related discipline cases, the rule pertaining to absenteeism is inadequate; it fails to inform the employee adequately as to what is expected of him or her concerning attendance. Similarly, contract provisions and verbal or written warnings requiring and advising employees to "become regular in attendance" or to "demonstrate an improvement in your attendance" do not, alone, constitute a proper discharge of the basic employer responsibility to inform employees of what is expected of them. Absent clear definition of such terms as "justifiable cause," "regular in attendance," and "improvement in attendance" and arbitrators have not hesitated to vacate, modify, or otherwise disturb attendant disciplinary penalties.

The First Step to the Solution of the Special Problems of Absenteeism Control: Reducing the Plan to Writing and Managerial Willingness to Modify as Necessary

There are many problems associated with more precise and specific definitions of absence-related terms. A case in point is the determination of the point of excessive absenteeism for the firm. Employee A may be absent 100 days during the course of the year, but if this is the result of a single lengthy illness (a nonculpable absence), termination may not be in order; Employee B, meanwhile, may be absent only 15 days, but this total may be considered excessive in light of the employee's reasons for absence (for example, culpable absences), incidence of absence (that is, number of separate instances), and seniority. In other words, simple measurement of the total number of days away from work does not define the point of excessive absenteeism. For these reasons, managers have developed various formulas incorporating such variables as total time absent from work, its scatter or pattern, *its causes*, the number of separate absenteeism incidents, and the absentee's seniority to be used as guidelines in determining the point at which an employee's absence from work becomes excessive.

Figure 8.1 represents one firm's attempt to bring the concept of excessive absenteeism into sharper focus and to advise employees clearly of what is expected of them regarding regular attendance. It is not presented nor intended as a model (or, for that matter, even a good) plan for absenteeism control but simply a step in the right direction as far as greater specificity of absenteeism-related concepts is concerned. The advantage of this plan and other programs[6] similar to it is that its shortcomings and weaknesses become immediately apparent as it is administered and enforced in the day-to-day operation of the firm, thereby permitting revision, refinement, and improvement of the control program. Like fine wine, the program will become better with age. Before this can occur, however, the control program and its key terms and concepts must be

Figure 8.1.
A Plan to Control Absenteeism

I.   A Point/No-fault disciplinary plan will be implemented
     as follows:

     A.   Points
          Absent (personal, sick, etc.)   1 point
          Absent without calling in   1½ points
          Late or leaving early less than or
             equal to 60 minutes   ½ point
          Late or leaving early more than 60 minutes   1 point

     B.   Elimination of Points
          1.   Regeneration--Perfect attendance for a 30-day
               period. Exclusions (listed in Section D below)
               are included in the regeneration cycle. They
               count as regular work days, except vacations,
               medical leaves, and leaves of absence. Vacations,
               medical leaves, and leaves of absence stop the
               30-day count, and it begins again upon return
               from these absences.
          2.   Points that are more than one year old from date
               of issue are automatically eliminated.

     C.   Points, Disciplinary Action, and Notices

Notice	Points	Action
White	3	Verbal
Green	6	Letter
Blue	9	Meeting
Gold	12	Meeting--2-week suspension*
Pink	15	Meeting-- Discharge

     D.   Exclusions from Point Assignment
          1.   Injured at work and sent home.
          2.   Jury duty.
          3.   Bereavement and qualification for pay.
          4.   Approved leave of absence (union, public, military).
          5.   Union business.
          6.   Special hours, arranged at least one day in
               advance and agreed to by supervisor.
          7.   Lack of work.
          8.   Medical leave--qualification for payment of
               accident and sickness benefits.
          9.   Fire calls.
          10. Vacations.
          11. Holidays.

*If an employee receives a two-week suspension and is subject
again to a two-week suspension within 90 days of the first,
he or she will not be required to serve another two-week
suspension, but will, however, receive the disciplinary step
and remain subject to discharge if he or she accumulates a
total of 15 points.

Adapted from: Auburn Gear Employee Handbook, Auburn, Ind.: Auburn Gear Inc., 1983, p. 4.

given concrete specification in writing. Although difficult, such specification of the point of excessive absenteeism and other absence-related terms and concepts would minimize, if not eliminate, the confusion that is all too often present in disciplinary cases stemming from poor employee attendance; it would clearly spell out for employees what is expected of them and thereby eliminate a major cause for arbitral reversal or modification of disciplinary penalties.

ARBITRAL REVIEW: WHAT ARBITRATORS REQUIRE IN ABSENTEEISM CONTROL

A study conducted by Professor J. Fred Holly of 1,055 discharge cases reported in *Labor Arbitration Reports* for the 14-year period from January 1942 through March 1956 revealed, among other things, that arbitrators relied upon the following principles to resolve grievance disputes:

1. Policies must be both known and reasonable.
2. Violation of policies must be proven, and the burden of proof rests on the employer.
3. The application of rules and policies must be consistent:
    a. Employees cannot be singled out for discipline.
    b. Past practice may be a controlling consideration.
4. When employees are held to a standard, that standard must be reasonable.
5. The training provided employees must be adequate.
6. The job rights of employees must be protected from arbitrary, capricious, or discriminatory action.
7. Actions must be impersonal and based on fact.
8. When the contract speaks, it speaks with authority.[7]

Managers should not only note but adhere to these principles in the formulation, promulgation, implementation, and administration of any program (that is, set of rules or policies) designed to encourage regular work attendance—in any program designed to control absenteeism. For, as the following arbitration cases clearly point out, these principles are as valid today as they were three decades ago, particularly where absenteeism-related discipline is concerned. The common thread running through each of the three cases as this arbitrator reviewed and ruled upon managerial action regarding poor employee attendance was the need for:

1. The formulation of clear and reasonable rules.
2. The communication of same to employees.
3. The use of progressive-corrective principles of discipline.
4. The administration of rules and the assessment of discipline in an objective, dispassionate, and evenhanded fashion.

Underpinning each decision was the working assumption that management retains the unilateral right to make shop disciplinary and safety rules unless otherwise limited by clear contract language or past practice.

Verbal Reprimand for Excessive Absenteeism

The Issues

Deitsch, Arbitrator—Whether the verbal reprimand given the grievant, K——, on October 6, 1982, for excessive absenteeism was for just cause and a violation of the contract. If not for just cause and a violation of the contract, what the remedy should be.

Stipulated Evidence

1. Joint Exhibit 1: Agreement between Square D. Company, Peru, Indiana and Miami Lodge No. 2069 of the International Association of Machinists and Aerospace Workers (AFL-CIO) September 14, 1981 to September 16, 1984, particularly Article II, Management Responsibilities; Article VIII, Leave of Absence; Article XIII, Grievance Procedure; Article XIV, Discharge; and Article XVII, General.

2. Joint Exhibit 2: *Handbook for Hourly Employees*, particularly Rule 4, Irregular Attendance or Habitual Tardiness.

3. Joint Exhibit 3: The grievant's written grievance, dated October 7, 1982, which reads:

I was given a verbal reprimand for excessive absenteeism. How can I be excessive when I followed our contract step by step. I have complied with the contract, and now I am being punished for such compliance. I did as written on page #25, steps 1, 2, & 4 per the contract. I ask that this reprimand be removed from my record and made whole.

Background and Facts

Square D Company informed its employees in October of 1981 that: "Effective January 1, 1982, we will consider total time lost from work, including leaves of absence not associated with work shortage, in our discipline program." (Company Exhibit #1.) Prior to this, leaves of absence had not been considered for purposes of computing absences, determining the point of excessive absenteeism, identifying problem workers, and assessing discipline designed to correct the problem. The policy change was prompted by an absenteeism level and attendant costs that the company believed to be excessive.

The grievant has extensively utilized the leave of absence during the last six years. His average of 130 days per year spent on leave during this period represents the highest average total time lost due to leave of any employee currently on the active payroll of Square D Company, Peru, Indiana. There is no question concerning the fact that the grievant did have legitimate medical excuses for the time off taken as leaves of absence from 1977 through 1982; among other problems, the grievant suffered from a chronic back ailment which, on two occasions, necessitated operations. In short, K——'s leaves were taken per the advice or orders of his physician.

The company communicated its new policy on absenteeism to the employees through normal channels—posting on bulletin boards and monthly meetings between foremen and employees from time of formulation of the new policy in October of 1981 through its implementation on January 1, 1982. The grievant was on leave of absence at the time the company initially posted its memo advising workers of the new policy. The grievant again took a leave of absence on January 12, 1982. It was at the conclusion of this absence on October 6, 1982, that K—— was verbally reprimanded for excessive absenteeism, thus prompting the instant grievance and arbitration.

Positions of the Parties

The following positions were taken by the company and the Union, respectively, in a hearing before the arbitrator on Friday, August 19, 1983, at the Square D Company conference room, Peru, Indiana and by posthearing briefs submitted to the arbitrator on or before February 7, 1984.

COMPANY:

Although this case involves a grievance filed over a verbal warning, it involves a much broader issue: whether the Company acted appropriately in including leaves of absence in its existing fifteen-year-old attendance control program effective January 1, 1982. As a preliminary matter, the arbitrator should summarily dismiss the Union's apparent claim that the Company was prohibited from modifying its rule on excessive absenteeism absent the Union's consent. In this regard it is most significant that the Contract in no way prohibits the Company from issuing or modifying work rules.

The longstanding principle that employers are entitled to issue and modify work rule absent express contractual restrictions is controlling in this case:

> The concept is well established in the labor relations field that, absent provisions to the contrary in the labor agreement, management may promulgate rules regarding employee conduct so long as adequate notice is given to the employees of the rule before it is enforced; the rule is reasonable under the circumstances; and the rule is enforced in a nondiscriminatory manner.

Ore-Ida Foods, Inc., 77–2 ARB ¶ 8377 at p. 4611 (Curry, 1977);

Accord Dresser Industries, Inc., 82–2 ARB ¶ 8329 at p. 4493 (Siegel, 1982) ("It is clear that an employer's inherent management right to establish reasonable work rules within the bargaining unit extends to an absentee control program subject only to applicable public laws and *specific limitations in the labor agreement*.") As will be set forth below, given the financial and production-related hardship placed upon the Company by excessive leaves of absence, coupled with the fact that the Company's lost time rate for leaves of absence was substantially higher than the experience of both other Square D Company facilities and those of other employers in the area, the Company acted reasonably and within its rights in including leaves of absence in its excessive attendance rule effective January 1, 1982.

The Union has not challenged the Company's testimony regarding either its excessive leave of absence experience as compared with other employers or the financial and production-related hardships placed upon the Company as a result of employee leaves of absence. The Union does not deny that filling a vacancy caused by a leave of absence can often cause production delays. Nor does the Union dispute that there can be literally a chain reaction of transfers occurring both when an employee goes on a leave of absence and must be replaced and when he/she returns from leave of absence to his/her old job. The main objections apparently raised by the Union to inclusion of leaves of absence in the Company's attendance control program are as follows:

1. Even if an employee misses a substantial amount of work due to illness, the Company should not be allowed to discipline employees because the reasons for absence are beyond the employee's control;

2. Disciplining employees for excessive time off due to leaves of absence violates the Contract's leave of absence provisions;

3. Since the rule on excessive absenteeism which has been in effect for at least fifteen (15) years does not set numerical standards, employees are unable to know in advance what the Company considers to be excessive absenteeism; and

4. The Company is prohibited from reviewing the employee's past record to determine whether he/she has exhibited a pattern of excessive leaves of absence, because this constitutes improper punishment of an employee for conduct which occurred in the past.

For the reasons set forth below, each of these objections should be dismissed as being without merit.

The Company, as well as most other employers, readily excuses occasional absences due to illness. The Union certainly cannot claim that the Company has unreasonably applied its revised rule on absenteeism with respect to leaves of absence or that it is using the revised rule in order to circumvent the leave of absence provisions contained in the Contract in light of the fact that only 7 out of 200 employees who took leaves of absence during 1982 received warnings. The question of whether employees can be disciplined for absences which have been caused by reasons beyond their control has been raised in numerous arbitration cases. The most common factual setting involves the termination of an employee who has a history of excessive absenteeism due to illness. Arbitrators are of nearly unanimous opinion that:

At some point the employer must be able to terminate the services of an employee who is unable to work more than part-time, for whatever reason. Efficiency and the ability to compete can hardly be maintained if employees cannot be depended upon to report for work with reasonable regularity. Other arbitrators have so found, and this Arbitrator has upheld terminations in several appropriate cases involving frequent and extended absences due to illness.

Cleveland Trencher Co., 48 LA 615, 618 (Teple, 1967); *Hawaii Transfer Company, Ltd.*, 80-2 ARB ¶ 4927 (Tsukiyama, 1980); *Husky Oil Company*, 65 LA 47 (Richardson, 1975) (see numerous citations contained therein chronicling this longstanding principle)

As these arbitrators have noted, although absences due to illness are unfortunate and in most cases beyond the control of the employee, *there becomes a point in time where an employer need no longer tolerate the uncertainties and hardships caused by the inability of a full-time employee to work more than on a part-time basis*. In the case at bar, the Company,has not acted arbitrarily or capriciously by summarily terminating employees who have had excessive time lost due to leaves of absence. It has incorporated its prohibitions against excessive leaves of absence within the framework of its long-standing five-step progressive discipline system for excessive absenteeism. The Company has consistently taken all absences, including sickness, in the enforcement of its rule against excessive absenteeism during the last fifteen years; the only change that it made was to include leaves of absence in consideration of when an employee has been excessively absent from work. By not previously objecting to consideration of absences due to illness in its attendance control program, the Union has given tacit approval to the very practice that they object to in this case—namely, disciplining employees for absences caused by reasons beyond their control. Leaves of absence for medical reason differ from occasional, daily absences due to illness only in terms of their duration; conceptually, they both involve absences for reasons beyond the employee's control.

Arbitrators have likewise entertained and rejected union claims that an employer may not discipline an employee for absences due to illness which were covered by a leave of absence, sick leave or similar provision in a labor contract. *See, e.g., Lutheran Medical Center*, 79–2 ARB ¶ 8565 (Cohen, 1979); *Central Sales Promotions, Inc.*, 74–2 ARB ¶ 8473 (Rey, 1974); *City Products Corp.*, 63 LA 148 (Yarowsky, 1974); and *Empire-Reeves Steel Division*, 66–3 ARB ¶ 8747 (Suagee, 1966)

The relevant portions of the Contract's leave of absence provisions, set forth in Article VIII, Sections 1 and 4, establish but two principles:

1. Written leaves of absence are required when employees are absent for more than three consecutive work days; and

2. Seniority employees *shall* be granted a medical leave of absence upon presentation of satisfactory medical evidence.

There is no restriction contained therein on the right of the Company to discipline an employee as a result of excessive time loss due to leaves of absence. Moreover, there is nothing contained in the leave of absence or any other provisions of the Contract to the effect that the granting of a medical leave of absence—something over which the Company has absolutely no discretion—is tantamount to the Company excusing or approving of the absence. The fact that a doctor may have certified that an employee was absent due to illness has never constituted a basis to "excuse" the absence with respect to the Company's rule regarding excessive absenteeism.

There is no doubt that on a case-by-case basis, such as is the situation with leaves of absence, the "no-fault" nature of the absence is taken into account by the Company in determining whether to discipline an employee. Indeed, most arbitrators have placed a greater burden upon employers who seek to discipline employees for their "no-fault" absenteeism. The fact that a physician certifies an employee as being unable to work due to medical reasons should be but one factor in determining whether on a case-by-case basis discipline was warranted—it should not, as the Union suggests, constitute the basis for an *absolute bar* upon discipline in such circumstances. In sum, the Union is asking the arbitrator to write into the contract something that is simply not there; namely, a prohibition on disciplining employees who have taken excessive leaves of absence.

Unlike some employers, the Company has opted to utilize an attendance control program that makes excessive absenteeism determinations more on an individualized case-by-case basis rather than pursuant to a point or similar type of system. As set forth above, this practice has been in effect for at least 15 years and has gone without objection by the Union. Indeed, during the proceedings in the grievance procedure preceding the hearing in this case, the Union raised no objections to this individual approach. (Tr. 15) In fact, the first time that the Union raised an objection to the utilization of an individualized case-by-case approach was during its opening statement at the arbitration hearing. (Tr. 4) This post-hoc attempt to bifurcate the Company's rule on excessive absenteeism should be rejected.

If the Company had adopted a point system for absenteeism other than those associated with leaves of absence and then promulgated a rule which generally prohibited excessive leaves of absence which did not incorporate leaves within that existing point system the Union might be in a position to claim that the Company has acted unfairly or discriminatorily in not putting employees on notice of what constitutes excessive leaves of absence. That was not the case here. The Company is simply considering absences due to leaves of absence along with other types of absences in determining whether an employee should be disciplined. It does not single out or otherwise treat them differently than so-called casual absences. The Union is certainly entitled to utilize the grievance procedure to challenge the appropriateness of discipline in a particular case. That is what it did during the past fifteen years of the Company's administration of the attendance control program. To require the Company to now issue specific guidelines in terms of days of leaves of absence, numbers of leaves, or some sort of point system in order to discipline employees for excessive leaves would not only constitute an infringement on the Company's management rights but also a substantial deviation from the fifteen years of past practice.

The Union's final challenge is that the Company is disciplining employees for past conduct when it reviews an employee's five-year history in determining whether he/she has exhibited a pattern of excessive leaves. Here, the Union completely misconstrues the Company's action. It has been the Company's practice to generally discipline employees for their conduct during the preceding six month period. (Tr. 29–30) As a result of this practice, the Union claims that the Company should be prohibited from reviewing more than the previous six months of an employee's record in determining whether or not he/she should receive disciplinary action. Plainly put, that position is absurd. There is a marked distinction between (a) *punishing* an employee for his past record; and (b) *reviewing* his past record to determine what disciplinary action, if any, should be given. In fact, the Company would be remiss in its responsibility toward its employees if it did not take an employee's past record into account. Restricting the Company in this manner would also likely work a hardship upon all employees. The Company cannot determine whether an employee has been absent an excessive amount of time, whether due to leaves of absence or otherwise, in a vacuum. In reviewing an employee's past record, it simply looks for some sort of pattern to determine whether the most present period of absences are an isolated event or are consistent with a past history.

The fairness of this review process is inherent from the fact that only 7 out of 200 employees who took leaves of absence during 1982 received disciplinary action for excessive leaves. By reviewing the past record, the Company is able to determine whether an employee is simply having a "bad year" or has demonstrated a pattern of excessive leaves over a period of time. This is a practice which works in the employee's favor—not to his/her disadvantage—and should be allowed to continue.

With respect to the particular facts involved in the decision to give a verbal warning to K——, there can be no dispute that he was absent from work an excessive amount of time. K—— had the worst attendance record in the plant. Up to the date of his warning, he was absent nearly 95 percent of the scheduled work hours for the year. All of the lost time during 1982 was attributed to leaves of absence. A pattern of excessive leaves is more than established from the fact that K—— has been absent an astounding 55 percent of the scheduled work days since 1977. In fact, since 1977, he has never been to work more than 41.4 percent of the time. The Company is simply taking the first step in the disciplinary process to put K—— on notice that being absent from work in excess of 61 percent of the time—making him less than a half-time employee—is a burden that the Company cannot and will not tolerate. The Company submits that this downright horrible degree of absenteeism is unacceptable and constitutes more than just cause for the issuance of a verbal warning. *Cf. Westinghouse Electric Corp.*, 39 LA 187 (McCoy, 1962); *Independent Lock Company of Alabama*, 61–2 ARB ¶ 81427 (McConnell, 1961).

For the reasons set forth above, the grievance of K—— should be denied in its entirety.

Stanley Weiner
Attorney for Square D Co.
FOLEY & LARDNER
777 E. Wisconsin Ave.
Milwaukee, WI 53202

UNION:

The primary issue in this case is the Company's establishment of a no-fault absence policy without consent or negotiations with the Union representing the employees of the Company.

Arbitrators have been faced with these provisions with increasing frequency in the last few years, and have displayed a good deal of ambivalence toward them. Arbitrator John Sembower accurately reflects the pros and cons of no-fault absence programs in Minnesota Mining and Manufacturing Co., 78–2ARB, (P–8461):

Finally, the Grievant was discharged under a so-called "no-fault" system of recording "occurrences" as automatically as possible. This kind of absenteeism control plan has found considerable vogue in the industry, and it follows in the train of similar efforts in the highly litigious fields of personal injury, domestic relations, etc. at law. The theory may be good that it saves much time and bickering not to go behind the "reason" for an absence but instead to call it a mere "occurrence." The trouble with this is that when the chips are down every reasonable person wants to know why, if possible, an employee was absent, and if it involves some very mitigating circumstances the reasonableness of counting it against him has a tendency to impugn the whole system. True, there are employees who somehow manage to get to work figuratively "through hell and high water," and Napoleon has been quoted as saying that what he looked for in a

General was a "lucky General." Still, if an employee really is flat on his back with illness and cannot come to the plant or his car is stalled on a frigid morning, it is natural for feeling of compassion to flow toward him. To hold otherwise is to make the employee "the insurer of his own presence on the job" and as a practical matter such a commitment is hard to swallow however nicely it may be accepted in the abstract.

Beyond the general assertion that management has the right to take appropriate disciplinary action to correct excessive absenteeism there is little unanimity among Arbitrators about the priority of no-fault absence programs. Most seem to agree that the no-fault concept involves in some sense an abdiction from Management's responsibilities imposed by the concept of "just cause" for discipline: to determine the merits of any event having disciplinary consequences.

Arbitrator William Duff has expressed this succinctly in *Robertshaw Controls Company*, 69 LA 77:

> . . . those "no-fault" plans which completely fail to distinguish between absences compelled by some unavoidable good cause and those which involve some element of culpability may, in some instances, achieve an abdiction of managerial responsibility inconsistent with the just cause standard. Evaluation of such plans cannot be conducted wholly in the abstract realm of principle, however, and the need to accommodate sound principles to the exigencies of everyday uniform administration of policy presents a very real, practical problem for Management. If a plan is fair on its face and its operation in the concrete cases at hand produces just results, and other common tests of reasonableness are satisfied, a plan ought not to be declared invalid based on the mere existence of some remote probability that it could operate perversely in the indefinite future under hypothetical circumstances which have not as yet materialized.

Given the ambivalence of Arbitrators toward a disciplinary program that seems to dispense with the concept of just cause is not surprising that several different approaches to the no-fault absence program have developed. One approach involves denying that the no-fault absence program constitutes any form of discipline. The most extreme example of this mode of reasoning is the decision of Arbitrator Eckhardt in *Gates Rubber Co.*, 68 LA 1273:

> It is important to note that the absentee control program which is being challenged by the Union is an administrative technique used by the Company to determine when discipline will be imposed, or considered. The initial imposition of points is not discipline; it is record keeping. The imposition of discipline follows the accumulation of a certain total of points. The imposition of discipline is still a judgment decision by management. That decision can be challenged by the Union in any specific case under the terms of the contract.

See also, Arbitrator Bailey in *Firestone Tire and Rubber*, 64 LA 1283.

The approach of both of these Arbitrators is to consider the no-fault absence control program as a form of record keeping without any necessary disciplinary consequences.

Both Arbitrators are careful to note that every disciplinary event must be subject to the test of "just cause" through the grievance procedure, and decline to limit the management in what they see as essentially a record keeping function which permits management to more accurately assess an employee's over-all attendance record. Both Arbitrators find sufficient justification for the record keeping program in the language of the Management Rights cause.

These two cases are open to the criticism that they must modify the concept of discipline in order to eliminate a disciplinary component in the "verbal warning." A verbal warning is considered merely to be "counselling," that it is possible to maintain as does Eckhardt that the no-fault program before him constitutes mere record keeping. The elimination of a disciplinary component for a verbal warning is contrary to the weight of arbitral authority, and is contrary to common sense in the Shop.

The Square 'D' management in this case has not contended that the stages in the plan prior to imposition of a suspension or discharge do not constitute discipline. In this case, Square 'D' openly states that the absentee and tardiness program is a disciplinary program at all stages of its application. (Tr. - 15.)

The majority of Arbitrators who have been faced with a challenge to a no-fault absence program have looked to the circumstances of the program and attempted to judge its reasonableness as a matter of substantive fairness to the employees. Characteristic of this approach are decisions by Arbitrator Seinsheimer in *Miami-Carey Corp.* 73–1ARB (P–8102), upholding a no-fault program; Arbitrator Herman in *Hoover Ball & Bearing Co.*, 66LA 764 (overturning the no-fault program); Arbitrator Cohen in *Park Poultry, Inc.*, 78–1ARB (P8420). In these cases, which go both ways, the Arbitrators have attempted to apply subjective criteria of "reasonableness" and "fairness" to assess the validity of the absence control program at issue under the Management Rights language of the Collective Bargaining Agreement before them.

Seinsheimer upheld a program which granted employees two and one-half "free" occurrences, which in his view would allow for a reasonable number of sick absences. Given the Company's "liberal" administration of prior excused absences and the existence of the "free" occurrence Seinsheimer found the program to be not unduly harsh and therefore justifiable. In *Hoover Ball & Bearing Co.*, Arbitrator Herman threw out a no-fault program which he found to be "too rigid and inflexible in not allowing excused absences for any reason other than those provided for expressly by the Contract at issue." The Program, in the opinion of Arbitrator Herman, essentially did away with the notion of just cause for discipline, and instead of waiting to apply the program on a case-by-case basis, he preferred to find the program unreasonable and therefore beyond the power of management under the Management Rights language. The reasoning is fully applicable to the present case.

In *Park Poultry, Inc.*, Arbitrator Cohen sustained the over-all validity of a no-fault absence program which he found to be within the power of management initially to promulgate and then refused to apply its terms to an employee discharged under the program for an absence which was beyond the employee's control. Arbitrator Cohen considered the just cause language of the Contract to override the terms of an absence program which was otherwise within the power of management to promulgate.

In still another approach to the problem of absence programs, Arbitrator looked to irregularities outside the text of the program as a basis for ordering recession of a no-fault plan. In *Minnesota Mining & Manufacturing Co.*, Arbitrator Sembower threw out a program which was unilaterally promulgated by management without consulting union officials, and which was never accompanied by any sort of formal educational program designed to inform the members of its requirements. Sembower sets out in the course of his opinion what he takes to be four criteria for upholding the validity of the unilaterally promulgated no-fault attendance program.

> The only issues really are the nature of a so-called "absenteeism program," and the manner in which it was implemented. This Arbitrator has rendered literally a hundred or more decisions in disputes such as this, and has studied hundreds of awards by other arbitrators. Out of this study, there emerge the following elements of an attenance and tardiness program: (1) That there be a clearly defined program; very preferably in writing. (2) That it be widely and fully announced and that every reasonable step be taken to see that it is thoroughly understood by supervision and employees alike. (3) That there be reasonable employee "input" both in the development and the carrying out of the program. (4) That there be careful, painstaking, and accurate record keeping including a recognition of that so-called "no-fault" systems while relatively simple to promulgate and operate almost inevitably lead to destructive misunderstandings which threaten not only the system itself but also relations between employer and employee.

> It goes without saying, of course, that such basic principles of disciplinary action as "even-handed" justice, due process, etc. are as applicable to absenteeism actions as to any other.

In the case before him, he held that the program promulgated by 3-M has been promulgated in a way likely to cause disruption of industrial relations and found that the disruption resulting would outweigh any positive benefits sought to be realized by management in a compelled reduction in absenteeism.

Arbitrator Sartain, in *Safeway Stores, Inc.*, 78–1ARB (P–8268), found in effect that the Company's unilateral promulgation of an attendance program which had been the subject of bargaining the past arguable constituted an Unfair Labor Practice and certainly required further negotiation between the Company and the Union.

In a set of facts which shows some analogous characteristics to the instant case, Sartain was unable to determine from the record whether the parties had in fact negotiated over the concept of "unexcused absences" and suspended operation of the program until the parties could reach agreement on the meaning of that language as found in the Contract before him.

In a case which is probably closest to the present case, Arbitrator Samuel Whyte held that a no-fault attendance program which contradicted the Contract in number of aspects was found on its own face as being beyond the power of management to promulgate. *Central Virginia Telephone Company*, 68 LA 957.

Faced with a management rights clause very close to the one involved in this case and a number of specific provisions of the Contract alleged to contradict the program, Arbitrator Whyte held that it was beyond the power of the Company unilaterally to change a fundamental criterion for just cause, without negotiation with the Union.

The disparate approaches of the arbitrators in these cases reflect a common threat of ambivalence toward the no-fault concept. Whether the Arbitrator sustains a program in general or throws it out pursuant to a general attack on the program, *all of these arbitrators seem determined to maintain the concept of just cause for discipline, and seek to confine management prerogatives under the management rights clause within limitations whereby the just cause standard will be maintained.*

With the possible exception of Arbitrator Eckhardt all seem to recognize, as does the

Company in this case, that what is proposed by no-fault absence program concept is a fundamentally new criterion for just cause, and seem determined to confine the operation of that new criterion within the narrowest possible limits.

In *Firestone Tire & Rubber Co.*, Arbitrator Bailey seeks to finesse the just cause issue by asserting that what management in effect did in establishing its absentee policy was to define what constitutes acceptable attendance, and thereby to establish a clear cut definition for just cause as it relates to lack of attendance. This is an unsatisfactory resolution of the program because it eliminates from the concept of just cause the notion of employee responsibility for the disciplinary offense which has traditionally been associated with the just cause concept.

While Arbitrators do recognize that an absolute inability to attend work and to perform that work satisfactorily is grounds for discharge, the accumulation of relative infrequent absences of short duration does not demonstrate inability to perform work.

Bailey's notion that the absence program constitutes merely a definition of unsatisfactory attendance for just cause purposes avoids the issue.

Sembower, Sartain and Herman seem to be most concerned that the introduction of the new concept of just cause be well understood by all employees and assented to (at least tacitly) by the Union. Significant in this regard is the weight which Arbitrator Cohen in *Park Poultry* gives to the acquiescence of the Union in failing to protest the implementation of the program for eighteen (18) months. It is clear from the opinion that the acquiescence played the major part in his decision to sustain the validity of the program. Similarly, Arbitrator Duff in *Robertshaw Controls* chides the Company rather harshly for attempting a no-fault program and makes it clear that, although he is rejecting the abstract "general" attack on the program, the program must be administered in accordance with the requirements of just cause.

This survey of cases occurring in the last few years sets out the framework within which the issues raised in this case ought to be viewed.

The Contract language involved in this case involves the intention to retain under all circumstances the notion of just cause for discipline is as pertinent here as it is in all of the recent no-fault absence program cases.

The language found in Article XIV Discharge states in the very first sentence "any employee may be discharged for just cause" thus it implied here that if the Company must have just cause to discharge they must also have just cause to discipline.

The Company takes the position that they have the right under the Management Rights clause to affect a new policy concerning absenteeism without the consent of the Union and the Company has never offered their defined program either in writing or verbally to the union for consideration, and to date no defined rule exists. The Company is attempting to gain something in this arbitration that they failed to gain in negotiations. For the Arbitrator to deny this grievance he would have to completely ignore the language of Article XVII, 4.

In summary the Company has failed to come to some conclusion with the Union about their contemplated and discussed plan to look at leaves of absence in consideration of absenteeism and now want that right granted them.

The Union objected to the exhibits of the Company concerning the grievant's record older than six (6) months prior to her warning. Again, we find that the Company admits that prior to January 1, 1982 they did not go back into an employees record more than six months in order to determine the level of discipline. (Tr. - 16). Unless as Mr. Mullikin testified that the employee was told in advance that future incidents of the same nature may result in discharge *then*, and the Union must assume only then, would the Company take that under consideration for imposing discipline. The Company failed to show that the grievant had been told in advance that his absentee record including leaves for the last *six (6) years*, not six months, was going to be considered, therefore we again object to the admission of Company exhibits showing the grievants record prior to 4–6–82. Additionally, the Union must contend that the change in reviewing employee record is and remains a negotiable issue and the Company failed to negotiate their desired change with the Union in the most recent negotiations therefore in the spirit of XVII, Section 4, the Union asks that the Arbitrator find that the Company has again violated the Agreement.

Finally, as previously stated, any rule that the Company chooses to promulgate must be reasonable and fair and to be reasonable and fair the rule must be closely defined, widely and fully announced, thoroughly understood by everyone, must have reasonable employee input in the development and carrying out of the rule and there must be painstaking and accurate record keeping. It goes without saying in this case the Company's rule change leaps out at you as not fitting any of those guidelines. What is the Company rule to date? The Union, the supervisor, nor Mr. Mullikin don't know, however the Company claims its rule is fair, but why shouldn't they, only they know what it is.

Summary and Conclusion

The Union respectfully requests that the Arbitrator find in favor of the grievant, K——, by ordering the Company to remove the unjust disciplinary action from his file and further by ordering the Company to stop its violation of the Labor Agreement by promulgating rules it failed to negotiate with the Union.

Charles Deppert
Directing Business Representative
IAMAW
5638 Professional Circle Suite 104
Indianapolis, IN 46241

Opinion of the Arbitrator

To resolve the issue in this matter, the arbitrator is called upon to make three determinations:

1. Whether the company is entitled unilaterally to alter shop disciplinary rules pertaining to absenteeism.
2. Whether just cause for the verbal reprimand existed.
3. Whether the discipline was arbitrary, capricious, disparate, or discriminatory.

Management's Right to Alter Shop Rules. The Union contends that contract provisions, specifically Articles XIV and XVII that address discipline for just cause and nonbargainable topics, respectively, prohibit the company from implementing a change in its absenteeism policy that includes leaves of absence for purposes of determining the point of excessive absenteeism and assessing discipline.

The Union's position is simply not tenable. It contradicts the "reserved rights doctrine" of labor relations law. "Reserved rights" is particularly compelling where labor agreements explicitly recognize the doctrine through a strong management rights clause as does the instant contract, namely:

ARTICLE II—MANAGEMENT RESPONSIBILITIES

1. The right of Management in the operation of its business is vested *solely* and *exclusively* in the Company and is *unlimited, except* as set forth in the provisions of this agreement. [Emphasis added.]

The doctrine holds that management retains all rights not limited by the collective bargaining agreement. That residual powers are retained has long been recognized by arbitrators.[8] Of particular interest are the following arbitral statements:

Arbitrator Harry J. Dworkin: It is axiomatic that an employer retains all managerial rights not expressly forbidden by statutory law in the absence of a collective bargaining agreement. When a collective bargaining agreement is entered into, these managerial rights are given up only to the extent evidenced in the agreement.[9]

Arbitrator John Day Larkin: Initially, before unions came into the picture, all power and responsibility in all aspects of personnel management were vested in the company and its officials. Except for certain limitations imposed by Federal, state, and local legislative enactments, there were no limitations on management's prerogatives. When a union is formed, and a collective bargaining agreement is entered into, the original power and authority of the company is modified only to the extent that it voluntarily and specifically relinquishes facets of its power and authority. . . . In short, the Company does not have to bargain with the Union to get "rights" which are inherent in the management function; but it may relinquish certain of those rights in the course of bargaining with the Union.[10]

Arbitrator Clarence R. Deitsch: Since all rights to manage initially reside with the employer (i.e., Appointing Authority), employees (i.e., State Merit Employees) derive their rights from the language of the successfully negotiated contract (i.e., applicable laws). All rights not limited by contract language are retained by the employer. In the present case, since there is no language in the State Personnel Board Rules limiting the Hospital's right to deny merit increases because of extended absences, the Hospital retains this right as long as other applicable laws are not violated. Appellant's argument would require the exact opposite interpretation implying that all management rights either pass "sub silentio" to the employees or disappear altogether—an unreasonable and untenable position in either case.[11]

Managerial prerogatives under the reserved rights doctrine, however, may be limited in several important ways. First, clear past practice may serve to amend the contract. There was no evidence whatsoever to indicate that management's right or responsibility to make, promulgate, and implement shop rules pertaining to absenteeism was compromised by past practice. Second, general contract language applied to specific cases may limit managerial discretion. Although it can be argued that the union's position constitutes this second type of reserved rights limitation, the arbitrator believes that it is best considered under the final category. Here, specific contract provisions may (and usually do) limit managerial prerogatives. Stated somewhat differently, an employer may not use reserved rights to destroy other rights specified in the contract.

The foregoing is precisely what the union claims has occurred in the instant case—that the company's decision to include leaves of absence as a culpable form of absence somehow conflicts with the just cause requirement for discipline of Article XIV and Article XVII's prohibition against bargaining either contract or noncontract topics for the duration of the labor agreement. This arbitrator fails to see any conflict between the cited contract provisions and the reserved rights doctrine that would limit management's right or responsibility to make, promulgate, and implement shop rules pertaining to absenteeism. Indeed, Article XVII, a so-called contractual "zipper clause," reinforces the reserved rights doctrine by removing contract and noncontract topics alike from bargaining for the life of the agreement, thereby leaving them to unilateral management determination, except as expressly limited by the provisions of the contract. Article XIV, in turn, is the only contract provision that could in any way be construed as affecting management in its role as rule maker. Even by the most liberal interpretation, Article XIV does not limit management's unilateral right to make rules, per se. It does, however, limit the nature and form that the rules may take as well as the manner in which they are administered. The following discussion addresses these issues.

Just Cause Limitation of Management's Right to Alter Shop Rules. It is incumbent upon the company to prove, *prima facie,* that the grievant, K——, was excessively absent from duty for the period charged—from January 1, 1982 through October 6, 1982. The quantum of proof generally required to establish *prima facie* cause in discipline cases of this nature is a "preponderance of the evidence." Accordingly, this standard will be used to resolve the instant grievance.

All employees will, on occasion, be absent from work due to illness. Managers readily excuse occasional absences due to sickness. By the same token, managers have the duty, the responsibility, and the right to protect their institutions from the harmful effects of excessive absenteeism. Termination of an employee whose poor health precludes regular work attendance is understandable, reasonable, and justifiable, given the need of an enterprise to efficiently accomplish its objectives. Arbitrators have traditionally recognized management's right to discipline (including termination) where employee absences have become excessive in nature, regardless of whether such absences were illness- or non–illness-related, excused or unexcused.

In the present case, there is no question in the arbitrator's mind that the verbal reprimand given the grievant constituted a good-faith attempt on the part of the company to guard against the harmful effects it perceived to result from the grievant's extended absence. A balance must be struck, however, between a company's right to protect itself from the harmful effects of irregular attendance and an employee's rights to know what is expected of him or her and to progressive or corrective discipline. This necessary balance was not struck in the instant case; the company, in its attempt to prevent or minimize the problems associated with absenteeism, compromised the grievant's rights by failing to develop reasonable criteria ("yardstick"—the term preferred by the Union) for determining the point where absences become excessive or having developed a reasonable criteria, failing to clearly communicate same to the grievant.

At first glance, the company's disciplinary action appears reasonable and justified. This conclusion would be the immediate response and natural reaction of someone focusing upon the one dimensional criterion for determining excessive absences: total time lost. Consideration of other criteria, however, muddies the water. The weight of evidence concerning the issue becomes more evenly distributed, possibly tilting toward "acquittal" (that is, grievant not being excessively absent), when such factors as the following are taken into consideration:

1. Number of separate incidents.
2. Cause of absence.
3. Scatter or pattern (pattern since rule change that became effective on January 1, 1982, in the present case—discussed below).
4. Seniority of the absentee.

That the company did reference factors similar to those noted is evident from the personnel manager's responses to the arbitrator's questions in this area; consequently, the union's claim that company had implemented and continues to administer what amounts to a "no fault" absenteeism policy (no fault in the sense that all absences, regardless of cause and other factors, are treated alike in a rigid and mechanistic fashion) must be rejected. Although its application of several of these criteria may have been incorrect, the company's "sin" was more in the nature of omission than commission—failing to give clear and concrete expression to the criteria utilized to determine the point of excessive absence. The just cause provision of the labor agreement not only requires just and reasonable criteria but that said criteria be clearly communicated to all employees. Absent said communication of criteria and discipline based thereon cannot be considered corrective or progressive, as required by shop common law. Employees must know what it is that they are to avoid, regardless of whether they subsequently modify or, in the case of illness-related absences, can modify their behavior in the desired direction. Simply notifying employees that, henceforth, leaves of absence will be counted in determining excessive absences does not discharge the company's contractually imposed duty to advise employees clearly of the standards being applied. With regard to leaves of absence, for example, an employee may reasonably inquire as to what the point of excessive absence is and the role (that is, what weight will be accorded to it) that leaves of absence play in calculating the point of excessive absence, to name but two possible lines of inquiry.

The arbitrator is fully aware of the problems inherent in determining the point of excessive absenteeism (that is, irregular attendance). Employee A may be absent 100 days during the course of the year, but if this is the result of a single lengthy illness, discipline may not be in order; employee B, meanwhile, may be absent only 15 days, but this total might be considered excessive in light of the employee's reasons for absence, incidence of absence (that is, number of separate instances), and seniority. In other words, simple measurement of the total number of days away from work does not define the point of excessive absenteeism. For this reason, managers have developed various formulas that incorporate such variables as total time absent from work, its scatter or pattern, its causes, the number of separate absenteeism incidents, the absentee's seniority, and the existence of "moonlighting" to be used as guidelines in determining the point at which an employee's absence from work becomes excessive. Although difficult, the gravity of the absenteeism problem confronting many firms warrants the effort on behalf of all parties affected. A proper determination of the point of excessive absence and the role of these variables would significantly reduce or eliminate the type of confusion and ambiguity evident in the present case, spell out for employees what is expected of them, and constitute a standard against which an employee's progress can be measured for purposes of determining appropriate disciplinary measures—all prerequisites for discipline to have its intended corrective impact.

The arbitrator, therefore, can only conclude that the company has failed to discharge its burden of proving by "a preponderance of the evidence" that just cause existed for the verbal reprimand given the grievant. Instead, the preponderance of evidence indicates that the verbal reprimand given the grievant, K——, was not for just cause—it was flawed and tainted by the company's failure to develop a reasonable yardstick for determining excessive absences that specifies the roles that leaves of absence and other variables play in the calculation thereof and failure to communicate clearly said yardstick to the grievant.

Arbitrary and Capricious Treatment: Retroactive Discipline. The company may protest that it did take into consideration the grievant's pattern and number of instances of absence in determining what it believed to be an appropriate penalty—that an average of 130 days per year on leave over the last 5 years is excessive by even the most reasonable of yardsticks. The arbitrator could not agree more. The question, however, is whether the grievant's use of leaves over this six-year period, while excessive, is also subject to discipline. The answer is an emphatic "no"! Leaves of absence only become culpable behavior on January 1, 1982, leaving a single incident and no pattern of use during the period of time for which the grievant was presumably disciplined—hardly the stuff that discipline is made of. That the grievant was disciplined for use of leave prior to as well as after January 1, 1982, is clear from the record. The company's own witness, the personnel manager, testified that, had the grievant not had a record of extensive use of leave prior to January 1, 1982, there would have been no disciplinary action taken on October 6, 1982, as was true in 208 other cases of leaves of absence in 1982. The simple fact of the matter is that leaves that were not subject to discipline prior to January 1, 1982, the date of the rule change, cannot become culpable thereafter in retroactive fashion.

In summary, it is clear that the grievant was held accountable for his use of leaves of absence for a substantial period of time prior to adoption and implementation of the rule change on January 1, 1982, treating leaves of absence as a culpable form of absenteeism. Such rule administration is clearly improper and patently unfair (that is, it conflicts with the just cause provision of the labor agreement)—particularly in view of the company's tacit, if not explicit, condonation of such behavior prior to January 1, 1982. An appropriate analogy, as noted by this arbitrator elsewhere and as referenced by the union, would be the levying of a fine upon a motorist in 1984 for having traveled 70 miles per hour in 1972 on the grounds that the motorist exceeded the 55 miles per hour limit implemented in 1974. Discipline administered in such a fashion is arbitrary and capricious.

Award

Based upon the stipulations of the parties, the evidence, the facts, and the circumstances of this case, the following award is made:

1. The grievance of K—— is found to be meritorious. Company's motion to uphold the verbal reprimand and dismiss the grievance is denied.
2. The company is hereby ordered to expunge any reference to or notation of the verbal reprimand from the grievant's personnel file.
3. The parties are hereby directed to compensate the arbitrator for his fees and expenses in accordance with the applicable collective bargaining contract.

Ten-Day Suspension for Being Absent without Leave and Failure to Maintain a Regular Work Schedule

The Issue

Deitsch, Arbitrator—Whether the ten-day suspension assessed the grievant for being absent without leave (AWOL) and failure to maintain a regular work schedule was for just cause. If not, what the remedy should be.

Opinion of the Arbitrator

A balance must be struck between an employer's right to protect itself from the harmful effects of irregular attendance (that is, tardiness, AWOL, absences) and an employee's right to know what is expected of him or her and right to progressive or corrective discipline. There is no question in the arbitrator's mind that a proper balance was struck in the instant case.

The facts indicate that the grievant has an attendance problem, manifesting itself on numerous occasions by a failure either to report for scheduled tours on time (AWOL — tardiness) or failure to report for scheduled tours at all (absences). Prior to the instant disciplinary action, the grievant was issued a letter of warning (reduced from a five-day suspension) on November 19, 1981 for being AWOL on November 6, 1981 and was assessed a two-and-one-half–day suspension (reduced from a five-day suspension) on May 7, 1982 for again being AWOL on April 26, 1982. After these two disciplinary actions, the grievant should have been abundantly aware of the importance of reporting to work on time *and* the consequences for failure to do so. Yet the grievant was again AWOL in October 1982—this time on two separate occasions. The disputed ten-day suspension was prompted, *in part*, by these attendance infractions.

As for the problem of excessive absences, the grievant was issued a letter of warning (reduced from a seven-day suspension) on May 7, 1982 for "failure to maintain required work schedule" (that is, failure to be regular in attendance) from January 10, 1982 through May 4, 1982. During this period of time, the grievant "had thirteen (13) instances of Sick Leave." As part of the Step 2 grievance settlement reducing the seven-day suspension to the letter of warning, the parties agreed that:

The Letter of Warning will be removed from record in one (1) year from date of issue *provided there is an improvement in the Grievant's attendance record and there is no further discipline in that period of time.* [Emphasis added.]

This put the grievant on notice that an improvement in attendance was expected.

Regardless of the nature of the yardstick used to measure improvement in attendance—total days lost, number of separate instances—improvement did not materialize. For the four-month period preceding the grievant's letter of warning on May 7, 1982, he had 3.25 occasions of absence per month (assuming the *worst* possible scenario that each day of absence was also a separate occasion of absence)[12] with an average of 3.25 days of work time lost per month (company exhibit 2). For the period of time immediately preceding the employer's disciplinary action precipitating the instant grievance, the grievant had 3.2 (4 ÷ 1.25 months) occasions of absence per month (virtually unchanged) with an average of 7.2 (9 ÷ 1.25 months) days of work time lost per month (approximately *twice* the previous amount). Rather than improving from time of issuance of the letter of warning in May of 1982, the grievant's work attendance actually deteriorated, per the widely accepted criteria noted above. The disputed ten-day suspension was prompted, *in part*, by the grievant's *continued* and *worsening* problem of irregular attendance. It is also worth noting that the grievant's absenteeism rate at the time of the subject discipline was 36 percent per four-week period—far exceeding one target rate of 5 percent consistent with the rate at which employees accumulate sick leave through employment (eight hours per month).

Given the nature of the grievant's attendance problems (that is, tardiness and absences) and the failure of lesser penalties to have the desired corrective impact, the arbitrator did not find the instant ten-day suspension unduly harsh or severe or at cross purposes with contractually required progressive or corrective discipline. To the contrary, the arbitrator finds employer's disciplinary action to be consistent with the relevant provisions of the labor agreement. It should also be noted that the disputed ten-day suspension for being AWOL *and* failing to maintain a regular work schedule is *less severe* than the combined discipline originally assessed for these same two infractions in May 1982.

The evidence is clear and convincing that the ten-day suspension assessed the grievant, C——, on November 5, 1982 for being AWOL and failing to maintain a regular work schedule was for just cause.

Award

Based on the stipulations of the parties, the evidence, the facts, and the circumstances of this case, the following award is made: "The Grievance of C—— is found to be *without* merit; *Grievance denied.*"

Discharge for Excessive Absenteeism

The Issues

Deitsch, Arbitrator—Whether the appellant's dismissal as an employee of New Castle State Hospital was procedurally correct and for just cause. If not, the remedy requested is reinstatement with back pay.

Stipulated Evidence

1. All procedural requirements specified for the arbitration of this matter were met.
2. Joint Exhibit 1: The letter from New Castle State Hospital, dated July 21, 1980, advising the appellant "of suspension pending dismissal on 8–8–80" because of a "continued pattern of excessive absenteeism."
3. Joint Exhibit 2: The employee complaint form containing appellant's written complaint and the written response of the appointing authority at Step 3 of the employee complaint procedure denying the grievance.
4. Joint Exhibit 3: The written response of the state personnel director denying the appellant's grievance.
5. Joint Exhibit 4: The written response of the chairman of the State Employees' Appeals Commission denying the appellant's grievance.
6. The appellant was absent from work 174 scheduled work days from time of employ-

ment on September 10, 1978 until the time of suspension pending dismissal on July 21, 1980.

7. The appellant's absences were illness related.

Background

New Castle Hospital is a state institution charged with the responsibility of providing care for severely and profoundly retarded patients. The appellant, J——, was first employed by New Castle State Hospital on September 10, 1978, as a developmental skills technician (that is, psychiatric attendant). Along with another developmental skills technician, the appellant was responsible for the direct care and treatment (that is, basic supervision to maintain the health and safety) of approximately 25 patients. The appellant was assigned to the midnight shift during the greater part of her period of employment with New Castle. On July 21, 1980, J—— was notified that, due to a continued pattern of excessive absenteeism, one of two alternatives must be taken, namely, suspension pending dismissal on August 8, 1980 or resignation for health reasons prior to August 8, 1980.

Positions of the Parties

The following positions were taken by the hospital and the appellant, respectively, in a hearing before the arbitrator on Tuesday, June 30, 1981 in the Brock Building of New Castle State Hospital and by posthearing briefs submitted to the arbitrator on or before Wednesday, August 5, 1981.

HOSPITAL:

I. Facts

J—— appeals her dismissal from employment as a Psychiatric Attendant at New Castle State Hospital. By letter dated July 21, 1980 (Joint Exhibit 1), J—— was notified by hospital Acting Superintendent . . . and the Basic Living Skills Module Director . . . , that she was suspended pending dismissal effective August 8, 1980, due to her continued pattern of excessive absenteeism. The letter also offered J—— the option to resign for health reasons prior to the effective dismissal date.

J—— was originally hired by New Castle State Hospital on September 10, 1978. From that date to the date of her dismissal less than two (2) years later, J—— failed to report to work on a total of one hundred seventy-four (174) work days or approximately thirty-five percent (35%) of the days she was scheduled to work. From September 10, 1978 to December 31, 1978, J—— missed eighteen and one-half (18 1/2) scheduled work days. For the calendar year 1979, she failed to report to work on eighty-four (84) scheduled days and from January 1, 1980 to July 29, 1980, less than seven (7) months, J—— was absent seventy-one and one-half (71–1/2) work days.

Included within the one hundred seventy-four (174) days charged against Petitioner are sick days (S), unauthorized leave days (UL), unscheduled authorized leave days (AL), unscheduled vacation days (V), unscheduled compensatory days (CO) and unscheduled holidays (H). The 174 day figure does not include scheduled days off such as scheduled vacation days, scheduled holidays and scheduled compensatory days.

Within these 174 days there were a total of 26 incidents of absenteeism. During her less than two (2) years of employment, Petitioner at no time demonstrated a consistent pattern of acceptable attendance. Petitioner's attendance record (State's Exhibit 1) reflects that during her employment at New Castle State Hospital, there was never a two (2) month period of time in which she reported to work on all of her scheduled days.

On four (4) occasions, J——'s attendance problem was verbally discussed with her in counselling sessions. On cross examination J—— acknowledged receiving three (3) of these counselling sessions namely, one conducted by her immediate supervisor . . . on April 12, 1979, one conducted by her team leader . . . on February 28, 1979 and one conducted by relief supervisor . . . on April 8, 1980. Petitioner's module director . . . also testified that he had verbally counselled her regarding her attendance.

By letter dated August 30, 1979 (State's Exhibit 2), J—— was notified that she had an established excessive absenteeism record. On May 1, 1980, Petitioner was given a formal letter of reprimand for taking four (4) unscheduled days off in the previous three (3) month period (State's Exhibit 3). In this letter, J—— was also notified that she had been classified as a "chronic offender." Following the letter of reprimand, Petitioner was again counselled in writing on May 21, 1980 for having an established pattern of excessive absenteeism (State's Exhibit 4). Finally, on July 21, 1980, Petitioner was notified of her suspension pending dismissal with the option of prior resignation for health reasons.

J—— declined the offer of resignation and thereafter appealed her dismissal pursuant to the procedures set forth in IC 4–15–2–35 of the State Personnel Act (Joint Exhibit 2). Petitioner's dismissal was subsequently upheld by the State Personnel Director following a thorough investigation (Joint Exhibit 3), and was further upheld by the State Employees' Appeals Commission following a full evidentiary hearing at which J—— was represented by legal counsel (Joint Exhibit 4).

II. Issue

Whether or not J—— was dismissed from her employment at New Castle State Hospital for just cause.

III. Discussion

J—— was dismissed from her employment at New Castle State Hospital effective August 8, 1980 because of excessive absenteeism. The overwhelming weight of the evidence presented at the hearing in this matter established that J—— had an atrocious attendance record during her less than two (2) years of employment at New Castle State Hospital. [The] Director of the Basic Living Skills Module at the hospital identified J——'s attendance record for the years 1978 through 1980 which record was admitted into evidence as State's Exhibit 1. The essence of [his] testimony was that from the time of her original date of hire on September 10, 1978 to her date of dismissal effective August 8, 1980, J—— had failed to report to work for one reason or another on approximately thirty-five percent (35%) of the days she was scheduled to work. This figure does not take into account regularly scheduled vacation days or other forms of scheduled days off.

[The Director] and [the] Superintendent emphasized that employee attendance has historically been a problem in the effective management of a mental facility such as New Castle State Hospital which by its nature required around the clock, 24 hour, 7 days a week employee coverage to tend to the needs of the institutionalized residents. The evidence also established that the failure of J—— to report to work when she was scheduled caused a staffing problem at the hospital with potential decrease in the quality of patient care.

Pursuant to Indiana statute and rules and regulation promulgated thereunder, all state employees are required to work (40) hours per week. Also according to state law, merit employees are granted sick leave at a rate of (1) working day for each full month of employment. The uncontroverted evidence in this matter established that J—— took well in excess of the statutorily allowed sick leave during her term of employment at New Castle State Hospital. Petitioner was employed at New Castle for a period of slightly less than twenty-three (23) months and missed a total of 174 scheduled work days by reason of her various illnesses.

Hospital policy C–3 (State's Exhibit 5) sets forth a progressive disciplinary procedure to be used in situations where an employee is absent without a physician's statement. Policy C–3 also contains a provision dealing with "excessive absenteeism" which encompasses situations where an employee is absent but such absence is documented with a physician's statement. This latter provision of policy C–3 was applied in the dismissal of J——, as it would have been pointless to progressively discipline her by way of suspensions from work since, according to her physician's statements, she was legitimately ill.

The applicable provision of policy C–3 provides that the Superintendent will cause a counselling to be provided the employee in an effort to improve the employee's attendance and that such counselling will be documented. J—— did receive such a counselling on May 21, 1980 (State's Exhibit 4) and, nearly three (3) months later was dismissed when her attendance did not improve. Thus, the requirements of hospital policy were met.

[The Director] testified that in applying the excessive absenteeism provision of policy C–3 he utilized a general formula which considered the incidents of absenteeism, the total days absent and the accumulated sick days of the employee. [He] testified that this rough formula was used by him in order to separate those employees with a few prolonged illnesses from those employees who missed work chronically. [He] also testified that he applied the above criteria on a sliding scale basis whereby for example if there are more incidents of absenteeism in an individual case than the threshold number, then less total number of days absent would be required to satisfy the general formula.

The attendance record of J—— reveals that during her less than twenty-three (23) months of employment, she accumulated a total of 174 days absent in twenty-six (26) instances and had zero sick days accumulated. From December 11, 1979, the effective date of the excessive absenteeism provision of policy C–3, to the date of her dismissal, J—— missed a total of eighty-three and one-half (83 1/2) days in eight (8) instances and had zero sick days accumulated. Thus, J—— fell within the general formula established by [the Director] regardless of whether one looks at her attendance record as a whole or merely looks at her record from December 11, 1979 to the date of her dismissal.

[The Director] further testified that he felt it would be unfair to apply his general formula by looking only at the hard and fast attendance figures of an individual for the

reason that such an approach would prohibit the administration from considering the total attendance record of the individual as well as any special circumstances which might
be involved. By utilizing a more flexible approach, each employee's case could be examined individually rather than mechanically resulting in a much more fair application
of policy C–3.

A case markedly similar to the one at hand was heard by the Indiana Supreme Court
in 1968. *Walden V. Indiana Personnel Board* (1968) 250 Ind. 93, N.E. 2d 191 upheld
the dismissal of a New Castle State Hospital employee who was dismissed because of
an unsatisfactory attendance record. The Supreme Court found that the employee's absentee record was excessive in that she had been absent 92 1/2 days in 1962. The Court
also found that the failure of the employee to report to work when she was scheduled
caused a staffing problem at the hospital and often resulted in a decrease in patient care.

The facts of the *Walden* case very closely resemble those before the arbitrator in this
matter. For the three and two-thirds (3 2/3) months she was employed in 1978, J——
was absent eighteen and one-half (18 1/2) days. For the year 1979, Petitioner was absent
84 days and for the seven (7) months she was employed in 1980, J—— was absent
seventy-one and one-half (71 1/2) days. Indeed, J——'s attendance record was worse
than the attendance record presented before the Supreme Court in the *Walden* case.

Finally, the proposition that J—— at the time of her dismissal was not healthy enough
to meet the conditions of employment at New Castle State Hospital is supported by the
physician's statement dated August 13, 1980 which she submitted to [the Superinten-
dent] at his hearing to reconsider her dismissal. This document, introduced into evi-
dency as "Petitioner's Exhibit 1," states that she was suffering from a chronic peptic
condition which was aggravated by stress. The statement further reads that Petitioner's
prognosis was only "fairly good" and that she needed "emotional counselling." "Petitioner's Exhibit 1" could certainly not have been construed by the hospital to be a
clean bill of health on behalf of J—— and provided no encouragement that her attendance problems as exhibited over the past two (2) years would be corrected.

IV. Conclusion

Regardless of the causes for J——'s absenteeism, the fact remains undisputed that
throughout her history of employment at New Castle State Hospital, she chronically failed
to report to work when scheduled. The hospital did everything in its power to correct
J——'s attendance problems and, having failed, was left with the inescapable conclusion that she was not reliable or healthy enough to maintain employment at the institution. The hospital's conclusion is amply supported by the evidence presented herein as
well as by the Indiana Supreme Court in the *Walden* case and the Indiana statutes relative to the care and treatment of mental patients.

Wherefore, New Castle State Hospital prays that the Arbitrator uphold the dismissal
of J—— as being for just cause.

Respectfully submitted,
Linley E. Pearson
Attorney General of Indiana

By: David R. Butsch
Deputy Attorney General

APPELLANT:

Issue

The issue to be determined by the arbitrator is whether or not the discharge herein was procedurally correct and if so, whether or not there was just cause for dismissal.

Summary of the Evidence

[The Director] testified that J—— was employed in 1978 and was assigned to an area containing one hundred severe and profoundly retarded residents. He further testified that she was a good employee, but that he thought she had missed an excessive number of days. He introduced her attendance record which indicated that she had an unauthorized absence on two occasions, February 24, 1979, and July 27, 1979. All other absences were properly authorized. He further testified that he had had others that had missed more days, but that they were persons who had suffered a job injury, an automobile accident, or those who had a lot of sick time accumulated.

He further stated that it was possible that someone could miss 200 days in a two year period and still not be dismissed. He testified he sent a memo to her on August 30, 1979, and a form letter to her on May 1, 1980. The May 1, 1980 form letter was in his opinion a reprimand and was delivered to her by certified mail while she was in the Henry County Memorial Hospital. He further testified that she was dismissed under Category 2 of Policy C–3 for excessive absenteeism. He testified she had a proper doctor's statement for each of her absences. He further testified that dismissal under Category 2 did not require progressive discipline. He felt progressive discipline would not really help, and it was just a matter of deciding who had been excessively absent. He further testified that she did bring a doctor's statement that she could now return to work, but that it was not accepted. He further testified that there was a provision in the Personnel Rules to require a doctor's statement showing a prognosis, but that none was ever requested by the State. He further testified she did get her merit increases, and that the only reason she accumulated the two U.L. days was that she failed to call in on those two days. He further knew that she was in the hospital when he sent the May 1, 1980 reprimand. He further testified that the possibility of a Leave of Absence was never considered. That Policy C–3 was revised in December, 1979, that the May 1, 1980, letter was the first review period under the new policy, and that he reviewed the last twelve months of attendance, even though it probably had only been in effect four months.

[The Superintendent] testified that this matter had been brought to his attention by [the Director], that they had counselled her on May 1, 1980, and that when her attendance did not improve, they dismissed her. That the reason for adopting the policy in December, 1979, was that they had a person dying of cancer and because that person would not resign, they were tying up a full time position on their Manning Table. That there was no written hospital policy and no guideline in the Personnel Rules. [The Superintendent] made no attempt to contact Dr. Webb to obtain a prognosis of J——'s condition, and did not know how the employees were notified of their alleged violation of Category 2.

[The Director] was recalled and stated that you could not tell the employees the criteria for determining "excessive absenteeism" because if you did, the employees would run right up to the final day and then stop.

J—— testified that she worked a different shift than [the Director], and only remembered talking to him on one occasion. She testified that her illness had been corrected, and since August 13, 1980, she could have worked a five day week without fail. She stated the counselling by her supervisor was a handing of [the Director's] memo of August, 1979 to her. She also recalled that a team leader may have talked to her about her absences sometime in 1979.

Discussion

We have by the admission of all parties concerned, a grievant who must have been a good employee, for she received her merit increases even though her Module Director classified her as a "chronic offender." In fact, the only two absences that were marked U.L. were because she failed to call in, and occurred prior to the adoption of Category 2. The State admits that no attempt was made to use progressive discipline. In fact, [the Director], after the adoption of Category 2, in December, 1979, merely picked out the worst offender and terminated her. No attempt was made by the hospital to assist her in any way to improve her attendance, or to do anything in the way of trying to salvage a good employee.

She was fired from her job at New Castle State Hospital, allegedly pursuant to Policy C–3. That policy is entitled "Employee Use of *Unscheduled* Leave." There is a Progressive Disciplinary Action set out therein, which provides for discipline from a formal letter of reprimand to and including dismissal. However, the employer admits that J—— was not dismissed pursuant to those disciplinary steps. She was not in jeopardy of losing her job for *un*scheduled absence. She was, the employer contends, dismissed pursuant to the last section of the policy, which is found on page 3, Respondent's Exhibit 4, entitled "Excessive Absenteeism." That section provides,

> Any employee who exhibits an established pattern of Excessive Absenteeism will have his/her attendance record brought to the attention of the Superintendent (Appointing Authority). The Superintendent will cause counselling to be provided that employee in an effort to improve the employee's attendance.
>
> Such counselling will be documented.
>
> On rare occasions, it may be necessary to work with an employee regarding, for example: obtaining agreement for extended medical leave, consideration of part-time rather than full-time employment, participation in disability programs and in extreme cases, voluntary or involuntary retirement.

The grievant first points out that the policy nowhere states that it is intended to apply to *scheduled* absences. [The Superintendent] testified that she had not gotten to the point of dismissal pursuant to the provisions pertaining to unscheduled leave. He contended that the problem was with scheduled absences under the policy. The only section of the policy that could possibly be construed as having to do with taking scheduled leave is the last section, quoted above. That section provides for counselling. No other type of discipline is contemplated thereunder. On "rare occasions" the following actions are allowed:

1) Extended Medical Leave
2) Part-time Employment
3) Participation in Disability Programs

In "extreme cases," the employee may be voluntarily or involuntarily retired. There is no provision for termination of employment for use of scheduled absences. The em-

ployer cannot justify the termination of J—— pursuant to this policy. J—— cannot re-
tire. She has only three (3) years of service with the employer. Therefore, if the employer is to apply Policy C–3 to use of scheduled time, it is limited to granting the
employee extended medical leave, part-time employment or participation in disability
programs.

There was no evidence that extended medical leave was offered to J——. There was
no evidence that participation in disability programs was offered to her. If we are to
proceed pursuant to Policy C–3, the only remaining possibility is part-time employment.
This was not offered.

Of the four options available to the employer under the policy, two were not offered,
and J—— was not eligible for the remaining two.

In conclusion, the grievant believes that the employer could not properly apply Policy
C–3 to her case, which involved scheduled absences. Assuming *arguendo* that the policy was applicable, she should not have been terminated. The intent of the last section
of Policy C–3 is to *work with employees in an effort to improve attendance*. The employer did *not* offer viable options to J——. The employer could have offered her the
opportunity to work with other residents, not as severely violent and retarded. This it
did not do. In any event, termination pursuant to the policy was improper, and J——
should be reinstated to her employment with all back benefits.

Respectfully submitted,

Charles S. Brown, Jr.
116 North Main Street
New Castle, IN 47362
317–529–1305

Attorney for Grievant

Opinion of the Arbitrator

To resolve the issues in this matter, the arbitrator is called upon to make two
determinations: whether cause for discharge existed and whether the discharge
was procedurally correct.

Cause for Discharge. It is incumbent upon the hospital to establish, *prima
facie*, the cause for discharge. The quantum of proof generally required in discharge cases to establish, prima facie, cause is clear and convincing evidence.
The latter standard will be used to resolve the matter at hand.

In the present case, evidence entered by way of testimony or exhibits incon-
trovertibly establishes that:

1. The appellant was absent from her scheduled work shift 174 days during the period
   of time from September 10, 1978, through July 20, 1980 (see State Exhibit 1).
2. The general formula developed by the director of the basic living skills module at
   New Castle State Hospital, to be used in determining the point of excessive absenteeism, was well designed and reasonable. The formula incorporated total days absent, the incidents of absenteeism, and accumulated unused employee sick days. The
   guideline distinguished between unexcused and excused absences only to the extent
   that the number of incidents of absenteeism was figured into the formula.

3. Whether the criterion applied in the appellant's case is total days absent or the director's formula, the conclusion is the same: the appellant had established a pattern of excessive absenteeism during the period of employment with New Castle State Hospital.

The evidence is clear and convincing that the appellant, J——, was excessively absent while employed as a developmental skills technician at New Castle State Hospital. Hence, the hospital had, *prima facie*, cause to terminate the appellant's employment with New Castle State Hospital.

Right to Due Process: The Procedural Correctness of Appellant's Termination. The appellant contends that due process was denied when the hospital violated universally accepted procedural requirements for discharge or termination. Specifically, appellant contends that the hospital's policy concerning absenteeism was applied in an inconsistent fashion, changed, unclear, not properly promulgated, and applied retroactively. The burden of proving violation of due process rests with the appellant. It will be presumed that the hospital's actions were in conformity with universally accepted procedural requirements until the appellant establishes by a "preponderance of the evidence" the contrary.

In support of its position of procedural violations, the appellant offered the following evidence.

1. The letter of "counselling," dated August 30, 1979 (see State Exhibit 2) from the director of the basic living skills module to the appellant advising that she had an established excessive absenteeism record and that "if improvement is not forthcoming *disciplinary action may be* required" [emphasis added].

2. That, despite a continued pattern of excessive absenteeism over the next three months (see State Exhibit 1) the aforementioned *disciplinary* action was not forthcoming, leading the appellant to the conclusion that the hospital was not serious in its enforcement of the absenteeism rules and regulations.

3. That the hospital changed its policy concerning excessive absenteeism on December 11, 1979 (see State Exhibit 5) and that the new policy was vague and confusing. In addition, Policy C–3 lacked proper promulgation, particularly to those employees with an absenteeism problem.

4. That, under the new general policy concerning excessive absenteeism, intermediate supervisors were given the authority to develop and apply individual criteria in determining when employees under their supervision would be classified as having an established pattern of excessive absenteeism. The specific criteria utilized by the director were never made known to the employees under his supervision nor was there any procedure developed to keep employees informed as to their absenteeism status, other than the letter of counselling referred to above. Indeed, the director testified that an employee could conceivably exceed the limit without knowing the limit had been exceeded.

5. That, despite its introduction by the hospital on December 11, 1979, the new policy was applied retroactively in the appellant's case. The director testified that the appellant's review period encompassed the months from July 1979 through May 1980—

six months of which fell under the old policy. The director further testified that it was the appellant's attendance record during these months, when viewed in light of his formula for determining excessive absenteeism, that prompted his letter of "counselling," dated May 21, 1980 (see State Exhibit 4).

6. That, despite the director's and the superintendent's testimony that the appellant was terminated for nondisciplinary absences (that is, under Category 2 of Policy C–3 which purportedly addresses the problem of excessive absences regardless of cause), the wording of the "counselling" letters to the appellant on August 30, 1979 (see State Exhibit 2) and May 21, 1980 (see State Exhibit 4) definitely implies disciplinary action. The former makes explicit use of the term *disciplinary*, while the latter advises the appellant that she has established a pattern of excessive absenteeism, in part, because of "total days off without prior approval"—a disciplinary infraction under Category 1 of Policy C–3. If the appellant's termination was a disciplinary action as the counselling letters definitely imply, she was also entitled to the progressive disciplinary procedures of Policy C–3—which she was denied.

The appellant presents a compelling case for reversal of the hospital's termination action. Of particular persuasiveness are the following points.

Lax Enforcement of Rules. The evidence clearly established that the appellant was excessively absent during her first year of employment. Equally clear from the evidence and testimony entered during the hearing was the hospital's lax enforcement of its policy concerning excessive absenteeism prior to the appellant's discharge in August 1980. By not imposing disciplinary action in a timely fashion upon further absences as hinted at in the appellant's counselling letter of August 30, 1979, the hospital appeared to condone the policy violation, leading the appellant reasonably to conclude that her absences were not viewed by the hospital as an employment-theatening violation of rules. Indeed, the hospital's letter of August 30, 1979, itself, reflected a certain degree of ambivalence toward the appellant's excessive absenteeism when it stated: "This letter should also serve notice that if improvement is not forthcoming disciplinary action *may be* required" (emphasis added). This statement leaves the definite impression that disciplinary action may not result even if attendance is not improved. Given such circumstances as these, management can turn to strict enforcement of rules only after giving clear and unequivocal notice to its employees of its intent to do so in the future. Absent clear and unequivocal notice, arbitrators have not hesitated to upset penalties imposed by management.

Clear and Proper Promulgation of Hospital Policy Concerning Excessive Absenteeism. On December 11, 1979, New Castle State Hospital adopted Policy C–3. According to the hospital, Policy C–3 encompassed two distinct categories of provisions governing absences. Category 1 provisions defined unscheduled absences and set forth progressive penalties for excessive use of unscheduled leave—culminating in employment termination. Category 2 provisions dealt with the question of excessive absenteeism regardless of whether such absenteeism was excused or unexcused. Suspension and termination under Category 1 were viewed as disciplinary actions for unscheduled leave abuse, whereas the steps contemplated under Category 2 (including termination) were viewed as nondisciplinary personnel actions. The former required corrective (that is, progressive) discipline, while the latter did not.

Policy C–3 involved more than a simple reduction to writing of policies in effect prior to December 11, 1979. The superintendent of New Castle State Hospital testified that the provisions of Category 2 were intended to replace the hospital's case-by-case approach of dealing with cases of excessive absenteeism. The director went a step further by testifying, "Prior to December, 1979, there was not a declared category of excessive absenteeism." Further supporting the appellant's contention that Policy C–3 represented a new excessive absenteeism policy and a departure from past practice is the hospital's statement in its posthearing brief that December 11, 1979 was the effective date of the excessive absenteeism provision contained in Policy C–3.

Constituting a new hospital policy regarding excessive absenteeism, Category 2 should have been clear, unambiguous, and unequivocal in both language and interpretation. Representing a departure from past practice (that is, lax enforcement of rules pertaining to excessive absenteeism), the hospital should have made every reasonable effort to clearly and precisely publicize and explain the new policy (that is, Category 2) and its method of implementation. The hospital failed on both counts.

Although the intent and meaning of Policy C–3 may have been intuitively obvious to its authors, such is not the case for the employee. The format of Policy C–3 gives the impression of treating only the question of unscheduled absences. The title, "Employee Use of Unscheduled Leave," fosters this impression, and the position of Category 2 (that is, excessive absenteeism) within the text of Policy C–3 does nothing to dispel this impression. Furthermore, excessive absenteeism is not defined in Policy C–3. Hence, given the title of Policy C–3 and its format, as well as the absence of any definition of excessive absenteeism, there is absolutely nothing, short of infused knowledge, that would let an employee know that C–3 applies to excessive absenteeism in general. An employee could reasonably infer that Policy C–3 was directed solely toward disciplinary problems of unapproved unscheduled absences. The reasonableness of such an inference is supported by management's own apparent confusion as reflected in the letter of counselling to the appellant on May 21, 1980, wherein the superintendent and the director refer to total days off without prior approval which defines unapproved unscheduled leave in Policy C–3 (State Exhibit 4). Additional evidence in support of the appellant's contention that the hospital's policy was ill defined and confusing was the time spent by the Hospital during the hearing attempting to point out to this arbitrator the separate aspects of Policy C–3. On more than several occasions during that hearing, the director used the adjective *complicated* in describing hospital policy and procedure.

The hospital also failed to publicize and explain the new policy and its new method of implementation to its employees—not that this could have been accomplished given the policy's inherent obscurity and vagueness. Assuming *arguendo* that the provisions of Category 2 were self-explanatory, the hospital still had the responsibility to disseminate widely and explain clearly the newly adopted policy—particularly, as in the present case, where the previous policy was not strictly enforced. Simple replacement of the old policy with the new policy in hospital policy manuals located at strategic points throughout the institution does not constitute the required publication and promulgation. As for the policy's promulgation through open employee meetings, the director testified that he was not sure whether excessive absenteeism was discussed or not.

Compounding the obscurity and vagueness of the hospital's general policy on excessive absenteeism was the intermediate supervisor's authority to develop, adopt, and apply individual formulas for purposes of identifying excessive absenteeism cases. The ultimate reasonableness of the director's formula notwithstanding, he had the obligation to inform his employees of the standards being applied. This obligation was not met purportedly because the director feared that employees would abuse the policy if applicable standards (that is, excessive absenteeism cut-off points) were made public. His rationale for not publicizing applicable criteria belies the same type of questionable logic behind the argument that auto emission standards should not be published because some auto manufacturers will just meet those standards but will not exceed them.

Retroactive Application of Policy. The director of the basic living skills module testified that the appellant's attendance record from July 1979 through May 21, 1980 was reviewed in light of his excessive absenteeism formula and formed the basis of his and the superintendent's counselling letter to the appellant on May 21, 1980 (State Exhibit 4). The letter itself states that the appellant's attendance record for all of 1979 through May 21, 1980 prompted the hospital's issuance of the warning letter. Whatever the period of time during 1979 included in the attendance review period, it is clear that the appellant was held accountable for her actions for a substantial period of time prior to adoption and implementation of the policy (December 11, 1979) prohibiting those actions. Such policy administration is clearly improper and patently unfair to employees, particularly in light of the hospital's tacit condonation of similar behavior prior to December 11, 1979. An appropriate analogy would be the levying of a fine upon a company for having violated smokestack pollution control standards in 1978 when said standards only first became effective in 1980. The hospital's argument contained in its posthearing brief that, disregarding the period of 1979, the appellant's attendance record following December 11, 1979 warranted the termination action taken is without merit. Arbitrators have long maintained that termination "must stand or fall upon the reason given at the time of discharge." [13] (In the present case, termination proceedings commenced at time of issuance of the letter of counselling on May 21, 1980.) If the letter of counselling of May 21, 1980 was incorrectly drawn, the termination action stemming therefrom was similarly tainted.

Corrective (Progressive) Discipline. Although the hospital argues that the appellant was terminated under the nondisciplinary provisions (Category 2) of Policy C–3, that termination was based upon excessive illness-related absences the overwhelming majority of which were documented by physician's statements, that progressive discipline would have been pointless, and that the termination did not imply any wrongdoing on the appellant's part, the letter of counselling of May 21, 1981 (State Exhibit 4) strongly implies otherwise. Specifically, that letter states:

In reviewing your attendance record for 1979 to present you are considered to have an "established pattern of excessive absenteeism" as referenced in New Castle State Hospital Policy C–3. The criteria use for this determination is a combination of *total days off without prior approval.* . . . [Emphasis added.]

The phrase "total days off without prior approval" fits the definition of unscheduled leave contained in Category 1 of Policy C–3. Having been so charged, the appellant was entitled to the protective features of the progressive disciplinary provisions of Policy C–3—which she was denied. Although the foregoing may appear to be a technicality, it underscores the state of confusion surrounding New Castle State Hospital Policy C–3.

In light of the foregoing facts and arguments, the arbitrator finds that the appellant did establish, by a "preponderance of the evidence," that serious procedural improprieties marked the hospital's termination action—improprieties warranting arbitral disturbance of the penalty imposed.

Conclusion. As noted at the outset of this opinion, managers have the duty and responsibility to protect their institutions from the harmful effects of excessive absenteeism. In the present case, there is no question in the arbitrator's mind that the appellant was excessively absent by any reasonable standard and that her termination represented a good-faith attempt on the part of the hospital to guard against the harmful effects caused by excessive absenteeism—with respect to proper patient care and in light of curtailed state resources. However, the hospital also has responsibilities to its employees. These include but are not limited to the development of unequivocal and understandable rules and regulations, clear and proper promulgation of these rules and regulations, and consistent administration and enforcement of said rules and regulations per widely accepted labor relations standards. In the present case, the preponderance of evidence indicates that the hospital failed to properly discharge these responsibilities.

Award

Based on the stipulations of the parties, the evidence, the facts, and the circumstances of this case, the following award is made:

1. The grievance of J—— is found to be meritorious. Hospital's motion to uphold termination and dismiss the grievance is denied.
2. Given the incontrovertible evidence of excessive absenteeism on the part of J——, the requested remedy of *reinstatement with back pay is denied.* Instead, New Castle State Hospital is *ordered to reinstate J—— without back pay* upon receipt of the award.

SUMMARY AND CONCLUSION

Barring specific contract language or past practice to the contrary, management retains the unilateral right to make shop disciplinary and safety rules. This right is consistent with management's responsibility to the firm's stockholders to operate the enterprise in an efficient fashion. Balancing its obligation to stockholders, however, is management's obligation to its employees, namely, that discipline undertaken to accomplish functional organizational objectives be assessed in a reasonable, evenhanded, and nondiscriminatory fashion and be corrective-progressive in nature. This is the interpretation that more than a generation of arbitration awards have imparted to the just cause for discipline clause found in the vast majority of labor agreements.

Nowhere is the tension between managerial prerogative and just cause—between the functional test, fairness, and corrective discipline standards for purposes of determining just cause—greater than in the area of employee maintenance of a regular work schedule. Here, the weight of arbitral opinion is that disciplinary rules governing absenteeism be understandable and reasonable, corrective rather than punitive, clearly and properly promulgated, and administered and enforced in a consistent, objective, dispassionate, and evenhanded fashion. The first step to the solution of the special problems of absenteeism control is the reduction of the plan (that is, absenteeism rules and regulations) to writing and managerial willingness to modify the plan as necessary.

NOTES

1. Owen Fairweather, *Practice and Procedure in Labor Arbitration*, 2d ed. (Washington, D.C.: Bureau of National Affairs, 1983), pp. 224–243.

2. *Stockham Pipe Fittings Co.*, 1LA 160, 162 (McCoy, 1945).

3. Fairweather, *Practice and Procedure in Labor Arbitration*, p. 243.

4. James C. Duff, "The Quantitative Monitoring of Absenteeism: Do 'No-Fault' and Just Cause Standards Conflict?" *The Arbitration Journal* (March 1985), 40:61–62.

5. Sumner H. Slichter, James J. Healy, and E. Robert Livernash, *The Impact of Collective Bargaining on Management* (Washington, D.C.: Brookings Institute, 1960), pp. 634–636.

6. One such program is the so-called no-fault absenteeism control program. The structure, operation, and advantages of no-fault programs are detailed in Chapter 9.

7. J. Fred Holly, "The Arbitration of Discharge Cases: A Case Study," *Critical Issues in Labor Arbitration* (Washington, D.C.: Bureau of National Affairs, Inc., 1957), pp. 1–17, quoted and reported by Slichter, Healy, and Livernash in *The Impact of Collective Bargaining on Management*, pp. 657–658.

8. For example, see Arbitrator Whitney in 53 LA 1078, 1083–1084; Belcher in 53 LA 410, 412; Talent in 52 LA 93, 96; Dworkin in 51 LA 1174, 1181–1182; Geissinger in 50 LA 792, 793; Larkin in 50 LA 109, 111; Solomon in 49 LA 370, 380; Oppenheim in 44 LA 274, 279; Kelliher in 43 LA 1006, 1011; Quinlan in 38 LA 714, 715; Emery in 37 LA 1103, 1104–1106; Bradley in 35 LA 306, 310; Deitsch in 74 LA 1090.

9. *Cleveland Newspaper Association*, 51 LA 1174, 1181 (Dworkin, 1969).

10. *National Lead Co.*, 43 LA 1025, 1027–1028 (Larkin, 1964).

11. *Evansville State Hospital*, 74 LA 1090, 1093 (Deitsch, 1980).

12. Such an assumption increases the possibility for improvement in any subsequent period.

13. Arbitrator Guthrie in 10 LA 117, 118; Also see Arbitrator Ray in 51 LA 1019, 1022; Roberts in 49 LA 1207, 1210; Williams in 49 LA 210, 213; Healy in 12 LA 108, 115.

9 Absenteeism Policy and Its Administration: An Advocate's View

James Redeker

Customs do not concern themselves with right or wrong or reason. But they have to be obeyed; one reasons all around them until he is tired, but he must not transgress them, it is sternly forbidden.

> Mark Twain
> *The Gorky Incident*

And oftentimes excusing of a fault
Doth make the fault the worse by the excuse.

> William Shakespeare
> *King John*, IV, ii, 30

The previous chapter sketched broad guidelines to be followed in the assessment of discipline as part of an integrated program of absenteeism control. Specifically, it was pointed out that disciplinary rules governing absenteeism should be understandable and reasonable, corrective rather than punitive, clearly and properly promulgated, and administered in a consistent, objective, dispassionate, and evenhanded fashion. The presumption was that adherence to these guidelines would preclude or minimize the administrative and enforcement problems that have historically accompanied implementation of absenteeism control programs—problems highlighted by the arbitration cases of the previous chapter. In this chapter, James Redeker presents a procedurally simple disciplinary mechanism suitable for implementing in most integrated programs of absenteeism control. Based on a concept of "no-fault," the procedure closely follows the guidelines set forth in Chapter 8. It should be noted that the term *no-*

The material contained herein was first published as: James Redeker, "Employee Absenteeism— An Unnecessary Problem," *Personnel Administrator* (April 1984) 29:2–10. Reprinted by permission from the April 1984 issue of *Personnel Administrator*, copyright, 1984, The American Society for Personnel Administration, 606 North Washington Street, Alexandria, VA, 22314, $30 per year.

fault, as used here, applies only to the enforcement mechanism of an integrated control program and is not necessarily descriptive of the entire program itself.

EMPLOYEE ABSENTEEISM—AN UNNECESSARY PROBLEM

Absenteeism and tardiness are often the most difficult problems faced by employers and the most common issues we handle in our representation of employers. Collections of arbitration decisions are filled with cases involving unsuccessful attempts by employers to terminate employees with horrendous attendance records. It is not uncommon to find arbitrators ordering the reinstatement of employees with 30 to 50 percent absenteeism records. It is even more common for us to counsel clients with complex absenteeism control policies but with 10 to 15 percent absenteeism rates. The usual explanation is that the employees know how to beat the system and supervisors don't know how to operate the system. As a result, hours of management time are wasted discussing how to curb this problem.

I confess to a certain degree of bewilderment over this issue. Of the 16 causes for progressive discipline, this is one in which even the most soft-hearted, soft-headed arbitrators agree: employers have the right to discipline and terminate employees who fail to come to work or are late. Why, then, do so many employers have so much trouble controlling the problem? After reading every absenteeism-tardiness case reported in the last ten years and counseling numerous employers, I have reached the conclusion that employers create their own problems by allowing their desires to be fair and understanding to block clear thinking. The primary issue becomes jumbled and the policy becomes both confusing and confused. Consequently, the solution fails.

Start from the initial dichotomy where many problems first arise. While there is universal agreement that employers have the right to terminate employees who do not come to work or are late, we all recognize that human frailty and acts of God—or the transit company—will cause all employees to be either late or absent, sometime. Consequently, while absenteeism and tardiness are legitimate causes for discipline or discharge, if an employer is to have any employees at all, some absenteeism and tardiness must be accepted and tolerated. For this reason, employers refer to "excessive" absenteeism and "excessive" tardiness as the cause for discipline or discharge, not simply absenteeism or tardiness.

Here begins the problem: What is "excessive"? How much is too much? When is an absence to be excused? Put another way, how can employees be fairly disciplined or discharged when absences are due to illnesses that aren't their fault? Then, again, how do you tell that an illness was legitimate? Doctors will give notes for the darndest things—especially when they have not even seen the employee to hear about the subjective ailment.

In my experience, it is how employers attempt to accommodate the human condition that is often the cause for the confusion that dooms their policy. In recognition of the fact that some absences cannot be avoided, some employers classify some categories of absences as "excused" or refuse to call them absences at all, at least for purposes of their absenteeism control policy. In doing this, however, new and seemingly more complex problems arise—some of which are unsolvable. How do you determine, for instance, that a reason for absence is legitimate? In trying to do this, supervisors are required to make impossible judgments based almost entirely on suspicious facts. Except when clear, objective evidence exists, such as an injury or hospitalization, there is always the possibility that the employee is pulling a fast one and beating the system.

I suggest that one way out of this mess is to reexamine the initial premise. Remember that what concerns employers is excessive absenteeism and excessive tardiness. However, what is "excessive" defies definition. Moreover, even when arbitrarily defined, excessive becomes impossible to administer on a case-by-case basis when concepts of legitimacy and excuses enter the formula. Absenteeism and tardiness, on the other hand, are capable of precise and easily understood definitions: if an employee is not at work, the employee is absent. If the employee is not on time, the employee is tardy.

When employers start to equivocate on the definitions of *absent* and *tardy*, I have found they get confused and impossible difficulties occur. By their own well-intentioned hand, employers do themselves and their employees a great disservice by increasing the variables from two to four, that is, all four concepts—excessive absenteeism and excessive tardiness—are left to definition on a case-by-case basis. In the process, employers need a computer to sort out the ways to handle the infinite factual combinations that can result. Employees become confused and convinced of unfair treatment. It is out of this confusion that discipline becomes difficult and abuse becomes easy.

The arguments I most often hear at this juncture usually go like this: "How can I term someone who is one minute late 'tardy' and still be fair? I am concerned about the employee who is ten minutes or more late. They are tardy. How can I mark someone who is legitimately ill 'absent'? I am concerned about the irresponsible employee who just takes time off."

If ten minutes is late, why isn't nine minutes late? Or six minutes? Or two minutes? Isn't late when you are not on time? Why draw the line at 10 minutes, or six minutes, or 15 minutes? What purpose does that serve? Do you really think that drawing the line anywhere but at the starting time changes anything?

In my experience, it makes no difference where you draw the line; the same number of people will fall on either side. On the whole, out of a hundred employees, five will be late no matter where the line is drawn. Why not, then, draw the line where it will do your operation the most good—at the starting time?

By the same measure, the same principle applies to the concept of absenteeism. It is finite and definable. Employers only confuse themselves and their employees by playing around with the definition. How can you really determine the legitimacy of an illness? However you choose to handle legitimate absences, I suggest you only generate unsolvable problems when you do it by manipulating the definition of absent. Absent is not being at work. Who can misunderstand or twist that definition?

Employers should restrict their differentiation between kinds of absences and tardiness—if that is what they wish to do—to the concept of excessive. Even when this is done, however, the deathwish of some employers is so strong that they cannot avoid creating unnecessary problems for themselves. This most often takes the form of calling some absences or latenesses excused and some nonexcused. The injection of excuses as a substantive part of the control program, however, frequently brings with it confusion and abuse. While the variables have been reduced to only what is excessive, the employer has solved nothing. What is a valid excuse? Obviously, there are some. The problem is which ones. Even when you can determine appropriate categories of valid excuses, how do you avoid abuse? There are a seemingly infinite number of factual circumstances that will place many cases on the fringe of an excuse category and many times employers find they cannot count an absence under their program because they cannot prove dishonesty.

Again, return to the initial premise. The human and natural condition dictates that, on the average, some absenteeism and tardiness is unavoidable. However, even when the absences are due to unavoidable events—legitimate illnesses, for example—there are some limits to how much absenteeism an employer must tolerate. An employee who cannot come to work a significant amount of the time cannot be productive and should be terminated, regardless of the reason for the absence. An employer may be more compassionate with an employee with a real medical problem, but, in the interest of the operation, this compassion can only allow so much absenteeism. These people can be put on a medical leave of absence or other devices can be used to treat them as special cases, outside the scope of the control system. The entire control programs should not be skewed to cover these cases. To do so ensures the unworkability of the system.

Removing chronically ill employees from the system and treating them individually ensures that the real problem employees are handled properly—those with single day or repeated short-term absences for multiple reasons.

The simplest system to administer, and the only one which I have found to be genuinely successful, is based on a concept of no fault. With such a system, the employer removes from all consideration (except fitness to return to work or medical insurance) the reason why an employee was late or absent. Employers establish the number of absences and latenesses they feel is sufficient to take care of the vagaries of life and establish a policy that any absence or lateness in excess of that number, regardless of cause, will result in discipline or discharge. There are no such things as excuses that have any relevancy to the system. Although such a system builds a floor of acceptable absenteeism and lateness, it is, as a practical measure, no different from what is caused by other, less conscious, programs.

In setting up a policy on this basis, the only questions an employer must answer are how many occurrences of absence and lateness over the course of what time period will be excessive and what system will be used to allow an employee to repair his record.

In a typical case—one like many I have assisted employers in designing and implementing—an employer may decide that 12 occurrences of absenteeism or lateness in a year will be excessive and warrant the termination of an employee. In this context, an occurrence is defined as any absence or tardiness (except those designated as holidays, vacation, bereavement leave, jury duty, leaves of absence, and so on), regardless of cause. Multiple days of absence are a single occurrence. Consequently, an accumulation of 12 occurrences in a year will result in discharge. As 12 months goes by from an occurrence, that occurrence becomes void. As a result, an employee is judged only on the 12 months following the first occurrence and can repair the record through good attendance.

A variation of this system is the elimination of the rolling 12 months and allowing employees to repair their records only through perfect attendance. With this system, perfect attendance for three months, for instance, will result in the dropping of one occurrence. Each consecutive additional month of perfect attendance thereafter will void another occurrence. The accumulation and voiding of occurrences continues without concern for other time periods.

Since the causes for the absence or tardiness are irrelevant, the focus is on the conduct and its effect on the operations. A premium is placed on maintaining personal health and means of transportation—legitimate employee responsibilities. Because the number of occurrences allowed is set high enough to cover a normal (perhaps an abnormal) level of human frailties and difficulties beyond the control of the employee, a judicious use of allowable absences permits responsible employees sufficient protection against unfair discipline. Because the system is void of any judgment calls, it is easy to administer, easily understood, and impossible to abuse, except for the initial stages of accumulation.

As fate and Murphy's Law would have it, however, the final occurrences that will dictate an employee's discharge will almost always be a *bona fide* absence or tardiness, that is, an injury, a hospitalization, a bus breakdown. The natural instinct is to excuse that absence and not discharge the employee. Employers always seem to fear that if a legitimately unavoidable absence is a precipitating cause for a discharge, an arbitrator will reverse the action or, in an organized setting, will be viewed as unfair by other employees. Those times are admittedly tough. However, it is also almost always the case that if employees are responsible earlier, legitimate absences later will not bring them to the threshhold of discharge.

For the system to have integrity and work, the employee in the example must be discharged. As a possible way to avoid the appearance of unfairness and the tendency to "give a break," employees must be given general and specific notices that the misuse of allowable occurrences places them in great jeopardy because there is no modification later and they cannot predict when something outside their control will happen. Again, the number of allowable occurrences is premised upon the belief that employees will be absent or late only when it is unavoidable. Consequently, responsible employees will stay clear of the trouble zones. The final and predictable action must be taken, even though it requires a temporarily hardened heart.

Even if all of the occurrences were legitimate, the employer must still uphold the honesty of the system. After all, the employer cannot afford to be burdened by sickly employees, and long before the discharge stage some action should have been taken to resolve the problem by a leave of absence or some other means that removes an employee entitled to accommodation from the system.

Of course, absenteeism and tardiness are the most responsive to progressive discipline and the no-fault system must have this element built in. Consequently, after a designated number of occurrences, warnings must be given and employers may wish at the tenth or eleventh occurrence to shoot themselves in the foot and give an employee a disciplinary suspension. Since the purpose of progressive discipline is to give employees notice of their violations and an opportunity to correct behavior, a suspension is of no greater value than a final warning. For that reason, there is real doubt about the use of a disciplinary suspension. Nevertheless, it is a traditional step sometimes found by arbitrators to have some special effect. Even so, the employer-caused absence is an employer-caused disruption to operations and there is some doubt about whether the hurt to the employer is worth the attention-getting value. I think not, and would opt for strong final warnings sent to the home as an alternative. Spouses frequently have more ingenious and effective ways of getting the employee's attention.

After years of arbitrating absenteeism-tardiness cases and working with employers to resolve their unique problems in this area, I am convinced that the no-fault system works if it is run the way it was designed to run. It controls the problem and ensures that discipline and discharge for violations are sustained for just cause. The key, however, is educating the employees and training supervisors. Without those elements, the system may lose its integrity and totally collapse.

10 Summary and Conclusion

The harvest is good but laborers are scarce.

Matthew 9: 37

Absenteeism is, in many respects, a by-product of the modern market economy—a co-product with a standard of living undreamed of by earlier generations—produced by the division and specialization of labor. The greater propensity to be absent in today's highly specialized and interdependent market economy is largely the result of the "push" of worker alienation stemming from the routine of simple repetitive tasks and loss of worker identity with the completed product and the "pull" provided by the higher standard of living. A higher standard of living may take the form of fewer hours of work or the form of increased real income. Both forms promote absenteeism, the former permitting the worker to cultivate a taste for leisure and the latter enabling the worker to purchase additional leisure as well as the means to enjoy it. Until mankind's understanding of absenteeism, its causes, and its methods of control expands and begins to approach its mastery of the physical sciences, future increases in worker productivity and, thus, the general standard of living are likely to be severely constrained.

THE PROBLEM

Absenteeism has proven itself a worthy adversary of managerial policy makers. Problems are first encountered in attempts to measure absenteeism. Quite simply, no universally accepted, single measure for absenteeism has yet been devised that adequately captures the various dimensions of the absenteeism problem. Each measure developed to date focuses upon some particular aspect of the absenteeism problem rather than upon its overall organizational impact. A number of different indices (for example, lost time index, worst day index, and frequency index), therefore, have been developed by practitioners and academicians to measure absenteeism's total impact for purposes of developing and implementing appropriate control programs.

Problems continue to confront investigators when they compute either firm-specific or the aggregate costs of absenteeism. These difficulties are due to the dual components of absenteeism costs, namely, explicit costs and implicit costs. Explicit costs are generally identifiable and can be expressed in dollar accounting terms. The explicit costs of absenteeism include:

1. *Wage costs*, including overtime premiums and wages and salaries paid to surplus workers who must be hired as replacements in anticipation of absenteeism.

2. *Supplementary benefits*, including benefits paid to absent workers and experience-rated premium costs of such programs as Social Security, Workers Compensation, and Unemployment Compensation.

3. *Costs of administration* associated with recruiting, selection, orientation, and training of the surplus workers required to replace absent workers and the costs of managing absenteeism.

4. *Production inefficiencies* caused by increased labor and material costs due to the use of less skilled workers to replace absent workers. Also, costs of production delays and the accompanying loss of revenue.

5. *Penalty costs* associated with scheduling difficulties because of absenteeism.[1]

Estimates of the out-of-pocket, explicit costs of absenteeism for the United States range from $8.0 billion to $26.4 billion per year. Stated somewhat differently, each day lost to absenteeism costs the American consumer approximately $66 in terms of foregone goods and services—output that would otherwise be available for purchase.

Implicit costs, on the other hand, may be defined as those costs that cannot be expressed accurately in dollar accounting terms. Absenteeism affects, in domino fashion, such intangibles as employee morale, discipline, and job satisfaction, which, in turn, increase labor turnover and reduce worker productivity, thereby reducing product quality and making production scheduling more difficult. All of these items may be termed the implicit costs of absenteeism. Though difficult to identify and measure, the implicit costs of absenteeism cannot be ignored in any analysis of absenteeism's organizational impact; they are a real cost of production, oftentimes more significant than the explicit costs of absenteeism noted earlier.

Measurement problems merely represent the tip of the iceberg. The factors responsible for absenteeism have proved similarly illusive, inscrutable, and difficult to analyze. A number of factors account for this: the sheer number and diverse nature of the variables influencing absenteeism, the myriad ways in which these variables interact with one another to encourage or discourage absenteeism, and the sensitivity of these variables to a wide variety of different environmental, organizational, and personal characteristics. Because of the magnitude, variety, and complexity of the variables influencing work attendance, practically every academic discipline has laid claim to absenteeism as its proper area of inquiry—proper subject matter for investigation. As a result, each academic discipline has developed, for all intents and purposes, its own theory or theories of absenteeism. The result has been the development of a body of knowledge concerning absenteeism that is a hodgepodge of disjointed, incomplete, overlapping, and oftentimes conflicting premises, hypotheses, and theories. Grouping various theories of absenteeism under five broad category headings—economic, psychological, sociological, jurisprudential, and disability—creates order from chaos by clarifying the assumptions upon which the theories sharing a common classification are based and by identifying appropriate remedies for absenteeism explained thereby. The five-category classification scheme cannot, however, be viewed as an integrated model of absenteeism because there exists a good deal of overlap between the five groups that cannot be eliminated due to incompatibility of terms, concepts, assumptions, and so on.

THE SOLUTION

A more productive method of combining various absenteeism theories to produce an integrated, practical, policy-oriented model of absenteeism control is along the lines pictured in Figure 10.1. Here, absenteeism theories are broadly classified as influencing an individual's capacity, willingness, or opportunity to work. This classification scheme reduces overlap and provides a more useful (realistic) description of worker behavior that is essential for controlling and limiting the harmful effects of excessive absences upon the organization.

The general model or theory of employee work attendance depicted in Figure 10.1 views regular attendance as a task accomplishment critically dependent upon an employee's willingness (that is, motivation) to attend, an employee's ability to attend, and an employee's opportunity to attend. The first of these important determinants of work attendance, namely motivation, is, itself, dependent upon two broad types of forces: job situational variables and internal or external pressures to attend work. Job situational variables can, in turn, be subdivided into job content variables (that is, the characteristics that define the job, such as job scope, level, advancement opportunities, and so on) and job context variables (that is, the job environment, encompassing such factors as role stress, work group size, leadership style, and co-worker relations). Job content variables appear to have a strong influence on both job satisfaction and willingness to attend work and, thus, upon absenteeism. Job context variables, on the other hand, although closely related to employee job satisfaction, have less of an impact upon employee work attendance. The influence of job situational variables upon absenteeism has led management practitioners and behavioral scientists to focus resources upon job design in an effort to create the kinds of jobs and job environments that increase employee willingness to attend work on a regular basis. In short, there has been a growing emphasis upon the development of jobs that improve opportunities for complete personal growth and development.

Internal and external pressures to attend work also play important, albeit not leading, roles in an employee's decision making concerning work attendance; they constitute important influences upon an employee's willingness to attend work regularly. The former include such personal characteristics as education, job tenure, age, sex, and personal work ethics. The last characteristic, personal work ethics, warrants further discussion because a decline therein—a decline in the Protestant work ethic—has been prominently identified as the factor responsible for the meteoric rise in employee absences. A more plausible explanation,

Figure 10.1.
An Integrated Model of Absenteeism Control

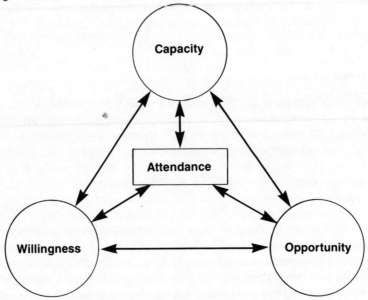

Capacity: The physiological and cognitive capabilities that enable an individual to attend work as scheduled.
Willingness: The psychological and emotional characteristics that influence the degree to which an individual is inclined to attend work as scheduled.
Opportunity: The particular configuration of situational factors surrounding an individual that enables or constrains work attendance and that are beyond the person's direct control.
Source: Adapted from Melvin Blumberg and Charles D. Pringle, "The Missing Opportunity in Organizational Research: Some Implications for a Theory of Work Performance," *Academy of Management Review* (October 1982) 7:565.

perhaps, is that there has occurred a change in what workers want and respond to rather than a decline in the work ethic, per se—that workers no longer respond to monetary incentives alone. If this is true, and there is no hard evidence to indicate otherwise, simple alteration of the reward structure including job redesign would go a long way toward correcting attendance problems.

The Protestant work ethic debate illustrates another important point: no clear line of distinction separates internal from external pressures that affect an employee's work attendance decision. For example, although personal work ethic was categorized as an internal pressure, it reacts and responds to the external stimulus (that is, pressure) of a changing reward and incentive structure as noted above. Other external pressures affecting the attendance decision that operate in close association with internal pressures are economic or market conditions and work group norms (peer pressure). Where the norms of a group, for example, emphasize the importance and desirability of good attendance, good attendance normally occurs.

The second important determinant of attendance, ability or capacity to attend, refers to the physiological and cognitive capabilities that enable an individual to attend work as scheduled. Variables that have an obvious impact upon ability are illness and accidents. Indeed, illness constitutes the single greatest cause of employee absenteeism. Not so obvious is the fact that personal characteristics influence an individual's ability to attend work. Personal characteristics exerting such an influence include accident proneness (some employers contend that certain employees are accidents waiting to happen), the ability to cope with stress, and age.

The final determinant of attendance, opportunity, refers to the configuration of environmental factors surrounding the employee that helps or hinders regular work attendance and over which the employee has no direct control. Two such environmental factors are the scope of family responsibilities and transportation problems. According to the ''competition for time'' theory, job and nonjob responsibilities compete against one another for use of the employee's limited time. Hence, to the extent that personal and family responsibilities demand more time than is available during nonworking hours or can only be taken care of during ''traditional'' fixed-hours work schedules, employees will allocate the necessary work time for such activities and, accordingly, absent themselves from work. Higher absenteeism rates for women with a greater number of dependents lends credence to this position. Transportation problems (that is, travel time, distance, and weather) also affect an employee's opportunity to work. Once assumed to be the sole responsibility of the employee, such problems have taken on added importance for managers in their attempt to combat high levels of absenteeism. As a result, managers have assumed a more active role in the solution of transportation problems.

This volume suggests an approach to absenteeism control that integrates appropriate economic incentives and rewards, disciplinary policies, and work environment modification. In essence, it is a simplified version of the integrated, practical, policy-oriented model of absenteeism control outlined in Figure 10.1 that focuses solely upon the variables that affect an employee's willingness to attend work on a regular basis. Specifically, the model provides positive incentives for regular attendance through the direct tying of both wage and nonwage economic benefits (that is, employee benefits, such as paid time off) to the actual number of hours worked and by improving the quality of the work environment through the methodic elimination or minimization of various sources of worker alienation: poor human relations, poor physical work environment, and unresolved employee self-actualization problems. Buttressing these positive behavior modification measures is a disciplinary system designed to eliminate undesired employee behavior (that is, excessive absences) through the assessment of penalties of varying degrees of severity. Unlike positive behavioral strategies, which attempt to elicit desirable behavior through systems of reward, negative behavioral strategies attempt to discourage unwanted behavior by punishing it through the assessment of discipline.

To effectively reinforce positive behavioral strategies in bringing about regular employee attendance and to stand the test of arbitral and/or judicial review, discipline must be administered in accord with several basic principles, namely: that discipline only be assessed for just cause; that penalties be promptly assessed to indicate clearly the connection between unwanted behavior and associated discipline; that the severity of any penalty be in proportion to the severity of the offense; that employees be clearly informed of all shop disciplinary and safety rules; and that discipline be administered and enforced in a consistent, objective, dispassionate, and evenhanded fashion in accordance with corrective or progressive principles of discipline.

THE PAYOFF

Given the magnitude and complexity of the absenteeism problem, a manager may understandably wonder whether programs modeled along the lines described herein work and whether they are worth the effort. The answer to both questions is an emphatic "yes!" The short-term absenteeism rate at General Motors has dropped substantially over the past few years, falling from 4.2 percent in 1980 to 3.2 percent in 1983. James E. Pryce, Assistant Director of Arbitration and Contract Administration, GM Labor Relations, credits a significant proportion of the reduction in absenteeism to implementation of a new comprehensive absenteeism program—a program strikingly similar to the integrated policy-oriented model of absenteeism control outlined and discussed in Chapter 5. The GM-UAW program provides positive incentives for regular attendance by directly tying both wage and nonwage economic benefits to straight-time hours worked. The program increases the cost to the employee for time spent away from the job, and, beginning with the 1984 labor agreement, it pays employees a bonus of up to $500 for perfect attendance. At GM, employee absences in excess of 20 percent of scheduled work during a six-month period of time reduce, in *quid pro quo* fashion, the employee's paid time off entitlement. When this is exhausted, reductions in other types of employee benefits are made. Any absences beyond the employee's control are not counted in calculating the 20 percent threshold number of absences that trigger benefit reductions. Final determination of whether an absence is culpable or not is made by a joint GM-UAW committee.[2]

An integral part of GM's absenteeism control program is its effort to improve the quality of the work environment through elimination or minimization of various sources of worker alienation. Prominent in this regard are the various quality of work life programs that tap employee input regarding the best way to operate lines, projects, or plants; improvied sickness and accident administration and prevention programs; and joint company-union counseling or counseling referral for those chronically absent as a result of medical, family, social, and self-actualization problems.[3]

Another example of the effective use of absenteeism control involves the adoption of flexitime—flexible work schedules that enable employees to simultaneously discharge both job and nonjob (personal and family) responsibilities. As noted above, according to the competition for time theory, these two broad classes of responsibilities compete for an employee's time. Absenteeism (defined to include tardiness) occurs when an employee cannot discharge nonjob responsibilities during traditional nonwork time. Flexible work scheduling permits, within bounds, an employee to tailor a work schedule that permits him or her to accomplish both types of responsibilities. Early research evidence tends to confirm that flexitime improves job attendance. For example, the results of a recent survey of the utilities industry conducted by Professor J. Carroll Swart of Ball State University revealed that the great majority of firms having flexitime schedules reported "very good" or "good" results as far as increased job satisfaction and reduced tardiness for clerical personnel were concerned. Specifically, Swart found that all firms experienced increased job satisfaction following the introduction of flexitime. As might be expected, therefore, 72 percent of the firms with flexitime reported either "much lower" or "somewhat lower" lateness levels. Although the results are less impressive with regard to absenteeism, 38 percent of the firms did report lower absenteeism rates while no firm reported a higher rate of absenteeism under flexitime.[4]

Some skeptical managers may still wonder whether the benefits of absenteeism control justify its costs. These skeptics should take note of the benefits generated by the GM project: approximately a $250 million reduction in operating costs during the first year alone. This figure does not begin to tell the whole story. James E. Pryce, Assistant Director of Arbitration and Contract Administration estimates that the joint company-union counseling component of GM's comprehensive absenteeism program was directly responsible for saving the lives of from 40 to 50 employees during its first year of operation. As these figures indicate and as in the biblical quotation cited at the outset of this chapter, there is much to be gained, but there have been few willing to make the effort—at least to date—with regard to reaping the benefits of a well-structured, integrated program for absenteeism control.

NOTES

1. Jeffrey Gandz and Alexander Mikalachi, "Absenteeism: Costs and Curves," *The Business Quarterly* (Spring 1980), 45:22–30.

2. Marjorie Sorge, "New Programs Slash Absenteeism," *Automotive News* (October 10, 1983): 3; "Labor Letter," *Wall Street Journal* (March 19, 1985):1; "The No-Shows," *Forbes* (April 8, 1985):10.

3. Sorge, "New Programs Slash Absenteeism."

4. Mary Zippo, "Roundup," *Personnel* (March-April 1984), 61:42–44.

Appendix: Agreement between General Motors Corporation and the UAW

MARCH 21, 1982
(EFFECTIVE APRIL 12, 1982)

MEMORANDUM OF UNDERSTANDING ON ATTENDANCE

Introduction

The Corporation and the International Union agree that the mutual problem of increasing unwarranted absences must be addressed in a cooperative manner. Both parties recognize that high levels of unwarranted absences are harmful to the business in terms of cost, quality, and efficiency and that the resulting stresses on the business constitute a very real threat to the job security of all employees. The Corporation and the Union recognize the unwarranted absences have an adverse effect on employees who do attend work and on the Union as well, and place unnecessary burdens on the Grievance Procedure.

Statement of Policy

Accordingly, both parties agree that there is a mutual responsibility to provide positive leadership for their respective employees and members, and that the following is an appropriate statement of that leadership role:

Unwarranted absence from work is recognized by General Motors Corporation and the International Union, UAW, as a breach of an employee's responsibility to attend work regularly in return for the benefits of employment and security afforded by the Agreement.

Commitments of the Parties

The Corporation and the Union agree that they will use their best efforts to achieve their mutual objective of minimizing the disruptive effects of unwarranted absenteeism on employees and the business. In that regard, both parties will explore innovative attendance control programs which may include initiation of and cooperation on matters such as special studies and pilot projects, which are designed to evaluate the causes, effects, and remedies associated with unwarranted absenteeism. Both parties agree to consider implementing, on a pilot basis, innovative alternative work schedules designed to improve attendance, to increase the utilization of facilities, and to reduce the effects of unwarranted absenteeism on the operations. It is understood that such innovations will be considered in light of the equities of both the Corporation and the employees involved. In addition, both the Corporation and the International Union will effectively communicate to their respective local managements and local unions their mutual commitment to reducing unwarranted absences among the employees.

The Corporation will assist its local managements in establishing and maintaining effective attendance control procedures. In addition, Corporation data on absenteeism will be provided for review and discussion by both parties to assist them in their efforts to improve attendance. The International Union agrees to actively support and encourage local union efforts in working cooperatively with local managements on attendance related matters.

Establishment of a National Committee on Attendance

Promptly following the effective date of the National Agreement, a National Committee on Attendance will be established. The Committee will consist of three (3) representatives of the Corporation and three (3) representatives of the International Union and shall meet periodically at mutually agreeable times and places.

The Committee shall be responsible for developing programs directed at reducing unwarranted absences and considering their effectiveness. Such programs may be recommended to local parties by the Committee as they deem appropriate and assistance will be provided as necessary to the local managements and local unions to implement those programs.

The Committee will explore and may approve innovative alternative work schedules which are designed to carry out the commitments of the parties as expressed herein.

In Witness Whereof, the parties hereto have caused their names to be subscribed by their duly authorized officers and representatives on this 21st day of March, 1982.

International Union, UAW	General Motors Corporation
Owen Bieber	Alfred S. Warren, Jr.
William Colbath	Byron P. Crane, Jr.
Maurice Treadwell	James E. Pryce
James Wagner	Larry E. Knox

MEMORANDUM OF UNDERSTANDING

Procedure for Benefit Entitlement for Employees with Irregular Attendance

During current negotiations, in discussions of the mutual problem of absenteeism, the parties recognized the basic principle that benefits are generated, earned, and funded by regular employment. Accordingly, a major factor in determining an employee's entitlement to these benefits should be regular attendance. In addition, the parties recognized that a small number of employees are absent from the workplace a vastly disproportionate number of days. Moreover, it is apparent that many of these employees have become adept at securing maximum benefits entitlement while at the same time protecting their seniority and avoiding disciplinary measures.

To address these factors, the parties hereby agree to a Procedure for Benefit Entitlement for Employees with Irregular Attendance. Under this Procedure, employees who experience controllable absences of 20 percent or more of available hours during an agreed upon base period will have their attendance rate calculated as a percentage and, thereafter, for the next six (6) months, the employees' entitlement to National Agreement benefits will be calculated by using this percentage as a multiplier. The National Agreement benefits that will be so calculated are as follows:

- Holidays
- Vacation Pay
- Paid Absence Allowance
- Bereavement Pay
- Jury Duty

In addition, for the next six (6) months, the employee's work schedule for the purpose of the administration of Exhibits B and C will be forty (40) hours multiplied by the employee's percentage of attendance rate. The benefits that will be so impacted are as follows:

- Sickness and Accident Benefits
- Regular Supplemental Unemployment Benefits and Short Work Week Benefits

In addition, the employee's eligibility during the next six (6) months for the Profit Sharing Plan, Exhibit F, will be calculated by using this percentage as a multiplier.

The appropriate National Agreement and Exhibits provisions are accordingly modified to effectuate this Procedure.

An outline of the mechanics of the Procedure is attached to this Memorandum.

The parties are specifically empowered to periodically review and evaluate the Procedure and make mutually satisfactory adjustments in the mechanics of its operation during the term of this Agreement.

IN WITNESS WHEREOF, the parties hereto have caused their names to be subscribed by their duly authorized officers and representatives on this 21st day of March, 1982.

International Union, UAW   General Motors Corporation

Owen Bieber   Alfred S. Warren, Jr.
William Colbrath   Byron P. Crane, Jr.
Maurice Treadwell   James E. Pryce
James Wagner   Larry E. Knox

ATTACHMENT A

Procedure for Benefit Entitlement for Employees with Irregular Attendance

Procedure Outline

- Communicate procedure
- A listing of all employees at each facility with a controllable absence rate of 20 percent or more in the following manner will be generated:
    (controllable absences)
    LESS (disciplinary layoffs)
    LESS (informal leaves) = controllable absence rate
    (available hours)   (a percent)
- To facilitate notice and a smooth introduction of the Procedure, a listing of employees will be compiled using data from October 1, 1981, through March 31, 1982, and those employees with a 20 percent or more controllable absence rate will be counselled regarding their rate of attendance and future applicability of the Procedure.
- Using data beginning April 1, 1982, through September 30, 1982, a 20 percent-or-more listing will be compiled by the Corporation.
- Designated Management-Union officials will purify list by removing candidates who have experienced major illnesses or injuries such as heart attacks, strokes, major surgery, etc.
- Put employee on notice
    - Effective October 1, 1982, under Procedure with benefits deductions for next six

months; while under Procedure, joint counselling efforts will be made to help employee correct attendance.

• During the first six-month period only that an employee is covered by the Procedure, the Corporation will counsel the employee in lieu of exercising its right to discipline for attendance-related infractions.

• The controllable absence rate (percent) established for the employee during a six-month period will be used to determine benefits entitlement for the next six months.

• When 20 percent-or-more lists are compiled, an additional identification of employees with 15 percent to 20 percent controllable absence rate will also be made and the employees on this list will be jointly advised of the potential for their inclusion in the Procedure should their attendance decline.

• At each six-month interval thereafter (April 1 and October 1)   establish the 20 percent or more list, etc.

• The intent of this Procedure is to address employees who experience the worst attendance levels in the Corporation. However, it is not intended that employees who experience legitimate serious major injuries or illnesses or employees who, over a span of time, have had excellent attendance records and experience a series of unforeseen or unexpected circumstances be adversely affected. In this regard, while not subject to the Grievance Procedure, problems with the removal of a candidate from the list, or with deductions made in the case of an individual where circumstances subsequently indicate that such deductions were inappropriate, may be discussed between the local designated Management-Union officers in an effort to resolve the problem. If the problem is not resolved locally, it may be reviewed by a member of the General Motors Department of the International Union and a member of the Corporation Labor Relations Staff.

Annotated Bibliography

BOOKS

Bellante, Don, and Jackson, Mark. *Labor Economics: Choice in Labor Markets.* 2d ed. New York: McGraw-Hill Book Co., 1983. A neoclassical approach to basic issues in labor economics focusing on the economic impact of the major institutions. The text uses basic economics as a foundation for analysis and discussion.

DeGrazia, S. *Of Time, Work and Leisure.* New York: Twentieth Century Fund, 1962. A theoretical review of the economics of the allocation of time. A theoretically rigorous treatment of how households decide to spend their time.

Dilts, David A., and Deitsch, Clarence R. *Labor Relations.* New York: Macmillan, 1983. An introductory approach to the problems of labor-management relations. The text includes an in-depth analysis of innovative approaches to conflict resolution based on basic economics.

Elkouri, Frank, and Elkouri, Edna Asper. *How Arbitration Works.* 3d ed. Washington, D.C.: Bureau of National Affairs, 1973. A study of reported arbitration cases focusing on the procedural and substantive aspects of the arbitration process.

Hammermesh, Daniels S., and Rees, Albert. *The Economics of Work and Pay.* 3d ed. New York: Harper & Row, 1984. A basic text focusing on the application of economic theory and statistics to the problems of labor markets. The text uses current data to demonstrate the operation of the labor market.

Hicks, J. R. *The Theory of Wages.* Gloucester, Mass.: Peter Smith, 1957. The classic work of economic theory and research analyzing wage determination within the framework of labor history. The theory of wages is integrated into general economic analysis utilizing the traditional models of the competitive environment.

Mabry, Bavars D. *Economics of Manpower and the Labor Market.* New York: Intext Educational Publishers, 1973. A basic labor economics text emphasizing market analysis as the mechanism for understanding job market problems. The text cites relevant literature and research to support its content.

Slichter, Sumner H.; Healy, James J.; and Livernash, E. Robert. *The Impact of Collective Bargaining on Management.* Washington, D.C.: Brookings Institution, 1960.

A classic and exhaustive study of literature, research, and case histories examining the impact of labor management relations on management practices.

JOURNALS

Allen, Steven G. "An Empirical Model of Work Attendance." *The Review of Economics and Statistics*, 63 (February 1981), pp. 77–87. A conventional labor-leisure choice model was adapted to generate predictions regarding variations in absence rates for a sample of individuals. Work attendance was found to be related to employee marginal earnings, perceived degree of occupation safety on the job, and flexibility of the work schedule.

Allen, Steven G. "How Much Does Absenteeism Cost?" *Journal of Human Resources*, 28 (Summer 1983), pp. 379–393. Mathematically rigorous measures of output loss to U.S. economy resulting from absenteeism.

Allen, Steven G. "Trade Unions, Absenteeism, and Exit-Voice." *Industrial and Labor Relations Review*, 37 (April 1984), pp. 331–345. This paper examines the effect of union membership on absenteeism. The results of this empirical study suggest union workers are more likely to be absent because of lesser penalties for absences and greater job dissatisfaction.

Atrostic, B. K. "The Demand for Leisure and Nonpecuniary Job Characteristics." *American Economic Review*, 72 (June 1982), pp. 428–440. Economic analysis of nonmonetary aspects of employment that are associated with a worker's demand for leisure.

Baum, John F. "Effectiveness of an Attendance Control Policy in Reducing Chronic Absenteeism." *Personnel Psychology*, 31 (Spring 1978), pp. 71–81. A report of a test of an attendance control policy based on a motivation pattern of legal compliance indicates improvement in attendance of chronic absentees.

Becker, Gary. "A Theory of the Allocation of Time." *The Economic Journal*, 75 (September 1965), pp. 493–517. A formal development of households as decision-making processes in allocating time between work and leisure.

Beehr, Terry A., and Gupta, Nina. "A Note on the Structure of Employee Withdrawal." *Organizational Behavior and Human Performance*, 21 (February 1978), pp. 73–79. A study to determine the strength and direction of the relationships among various types of employee withdrawal from organizations (psychological withdrawal, lateness, absenteeism, and turnover).

Breaugh, James A. "Relationships between Recruiting Sources and Employee Performance, Absenteeism, and Work Attitudes." *Academy of Management Journal*, 24 (March 1981), pp. 142–147. A field study designed to determine whether the sources through which employees are recruited are related to subsequent job performance, absenteeism, and work attitudes found strong source-of-recruitment effects.

Carlson, John G. and Hill, Kenneth D. "The Effect of Gaming on Attendance and Attitude." *Personnel Psychology*, 35 (Spring 1982), pp. 63–73. A study of the use of gaming to reduce absenteeism and tardiness shows limited direct impact but some improvement in employee attitudes and cooperation when gaming was used as a vehicle of communication.

Cheloha, Randall, and Farr, James L. "Absenteeism, Job Involvement, and Job Satisfaction in an Organizational Setting." *Journal of Applied Psychology*, 65, 4 (1980), pp. 467–473. Partial correlation analysis of measures of job satisfaction, job involvement, and absenteeism revealed that the relationship between job satisfaction and absenteeism was mediated by job involvement.

Dalton, Dan R., and Perry, James L. "Absenteeism and the Collective Bargaining Agreement: An Empirical Test." *Academy of Management Journal*, 24 (June 1981), pp. 425–431. An empirical study supporting the hypothesis that certain collective bargaining contract policies have the effect of making absenteeism easier and more profitable for employees.

Deitsch, Clarence R., and Dilts, David A. "Getting Absent Workers Back on the Job: The Case of General Motors," *Business Horizons*, 24 (September/October 1981), pp. 51–58. An in-depth examination of the compensatory provisions of the GM-UAW contract and overall contract administration policy that indicates that excessive absenteeism may simply be rational employee response to contractually structured and/or administered incentives to stay away from the job.

Dittirch, John E., and Carrell, Michael R. "Organizational Equity Perceptions, Employee Job Satisfaction, and Departmental Absence and Turnover Rates," *Organizational Behavior and Human Performance*, 24 (August 1979), pp. 29–40. A longitudinal field study examining the association between employee job satisfaction and perceptions of equitable treatment as they relate to absence and turnover.

Edwards, P. K. "Attachment to Work and Absence Behavior," *Human Relations*, 32 (December 1979), pp. 1065–1080. A study of the difference in absence behavior of "stayers" and "leavers" focusing on factors affecting attachment to work, especially length of service and reasons for leaving.

Edwards, P., and Scullion, H. "Does Sick Pay Encourage Absenteeism?" *Personnel Management*, 11 (July 1979), pp. 32–35. A controlled case study of the impact of a new pay scheme on a large engineering company's employee absenteeism.

Fitzgibbons, Dale, and Moch, Michael. "Employee Absenteeism: A Multivariate Analysis with Replications." *Organizational Behavior and Human Performance*, 26 (December 1980), pp. 349–372. An analysis of a multivariate model of absence behavior that distinguishes among excused and unexcused absences and absences attributed to illness. It also assesses the model at two different points in time.

Garrison, K. R., and Muchinsky, P. M. "Attitudinal and Biographical Predictors of Incidental Absenteeism." *Journal of Vocational Behavior*, 10 (April 1977), pp. 221–230. A study to predict two measures of incidental employee absenteeism (absenteeism with and without pay) using seven biographical and six attitudinal variables. The results indicated that paid absences were fairly predictable, while unpaid absences could be predicted to some degree by certain variables.

Gupta, Nina, and Beehr, Terry A. "Job Stress and Employee Behaviors." *Organizational Behavior and Human Performance*, 23 (June 1979), pp. 373–387. A study of the relationship between job stresses (role ambiguity, role overload, underutilization of skills, and resource inadequacy) with employee withdrawal behaviors (absenteeism and turnover). Job stress was found to be related to employee withdrawal behaviors.

Igen, Daniel R., and Hollenback, John H. "The Role of Job Satisfaction in Absence Behavior." *Organizational Behavior and Human Performance*, 19 (June 1977), pp. 148–161. An experimental study of the impact of internal and external pressures and demographic variables on the relationship between job satisfaction and attendance.

Jamal, Muhammad. "Shift Work Related to Job Attitudes, Social Participation and Withdrawal Behavior: A Study of Nurses and Industrial Workers." *Personnel Psychology*, 34 (Autumn 1981), pp. 535–547. A study investigating the relationship between shift schedules and mental health, job satisfaction, social participation, organizational commitment, anticipated turnover, absenteeism, and tardiness among nurses in two hospitals and among rank-and-file workers in manufacturing.

Johns, Gary. "Attitudinal and Nonattitudinal Predictors of Two Forms of Absence from Work." *Organizational Behavior and Human Performance*, 22 (December 1978), pp. 431–444. Research examining the relationship between two forms of absence from work (frequency of absence and time lost) and four separate groups of predictors (job satisfaction, personal characteristics, leadership style, and job content).

Johns, Gary. "Task Moderators of the Relationship between Leadership Style and Subordinate Responses." *Academy of Mangement Journal*, 21 (June 1978), pp. 319–325. A study of moderator effects of a number of task characteristics on perceived leader behavior and a variety of outcomes such as employee absenteeism.

Leigh, J. Paul. "Sex Differences in Absenteeism." *Industrial Relations*, 22 (Fall 1983), pp. 349–361. This article discusses an eclectic theory of worker absenteeism and develops a model to test a number of variables. Findings state that sex differences in absenteeism have been overstated. When alternative assumptions concerning men's and women's behavior and characteristics are made, the evidence suggests that if the endowments of each (such as wage earned) and responses to those endowments (such as child care) were more similar, the disparity in absence rates would narrow considerably.

Mabry, B. D. "Income-Leisure Analysis and the Salaried Professional." *Industrial Relations*, 8 (February 1969), pp. 162–173. A formal analysis of the allocation of time between work and leisure for white collar employees.

Markham, Steven E.; Dansereau, Jr., Fred; Alutto, Joseph A. "Female vs. Male Absence Rates: A Temporal Analysis." *Personnel Psychology*, 35 (Summer 1982), pp. 371–382. A report of a test of the importance of temporal trends within absenteeism data for males and females.

Markham, Steven E.; Dansereau, Jr., Fred; and Alutto, Joseph A. "Group Size and Absenteeism Rates: A Longitudinal Analysis." *Academy of Management Journal*, 25 (December 1982), pp. 921–927. An empirical longitudinal study of absenteeism in various sized groups with emphasis on the variation in the size of each group as an indicator of relative growth.

Mowday, Richard T., and Spencer, Daniel E. "The Influence of Task and Personality Characteristics on Employee Turnover and Absenteeism Incidents." *Academy of Management Journal*, 24 (September 1981), pp. 634–642. A study of the impact of job scope on withdrawal behavior suggesting the need to include situational variables that constrain or promote employee effective reactions.

Muchinsky, Paul M. "Employee Absenteeism: A Review of the Literature." *Journal of Vocational Behavior*, 10 (June 1977), pp. 316–340. A review of the literature on employee absenteeism as a form of withdrawal behavior apart from turnover.

Studies reviewing psychometric properties of absence measures as well as the relationship between absenteeism and personal, attitudinal, and social variables.

Nicholson, N. "Absence Behavior and Attendance Motivation: A Conceptual Synthesis." *Journal of Management Studies*, 14 (October 1977), pp. 231–252. This paper proposes a new model and associated methodology for the analysis and prediction of employee absence. It also provides a review of existing theory and suggests the need for an all new approach involving absence-inducing events and personality variables. Individual motivation to attend measured in terms of attachment is a key variable.

Nicholson, N.; Brown, C. A.; and Chadwick-Jones, J. K. "Absence from Work and Personal Characteristics." *Journal of Applied Psychology*, 62 (June 1977), pp. 319–327. A review of the literature on the relationship between absence and age and length of service in terms of differences between results of various absence types, sex of employee, and research design.

Nicholson, N.; Jackson, P.; and Howes, G. "Shiftwork and Absence: An Analysis of Temporal Trends." *Journal of Occupational Psychology*, 51 (June 1978), pp. 127–137. A study of the independent effects of shift turn, days of the week, and position in the shift cycle and their interaction on absenteeism. Each of these variables was found to have a significant impact on uncertified employee absenteeism in the steel industry.

Popp, Paul O. "Absenteeism in a Low Status Work Environment." *Academy of Management Journal*, 25 (September 1982), pp. 677–683. A review and criticism of current research literature on absenteeism for faulty methodology and inappropriate assumptions. A study of different measures of absenteeism and the impact of work and varying work group composition.

Robertson, D. E.; Johnson, R. D.; and Bethke, A. L. "Reducing Absenteeism with Fixed and Variable Interval Reinforcement." *Review of Business and Economics Research*, 15–16 (Spring 1980), pp. 73–82. An experimental study of the effect of varying reinforcement methodologies on employee absenteeism.

Rothman, Miriam. "Can Alternatives to Sick Pay Plans Reduce Absenteeism?" *Personnel Journal*, 60 (October 1981), pp. 788–790. A review of traditional sick pay plans that provide income during short periods of illness and the substitution of well pay plans that provide positive rewards for maintaining good health and work attendance records.

Shoemaker, Judy, and Reid, Dennis H. "Decreasing Chronic Absenteeism among Institutional Staff: Effects of a Low-Cost Attendance Program." *Journal of Organizational Behavior Management*, 2 (Fall 1980), pp. 317–328. A study of the effects of a behavioral attendance program on the absences of chronic attendance abusers in a state institution. The program involved supervisory counseling, letters of commendation for achieving desired attendance levels, and a behavioral lottery system and was successful in reducing chronic absenteeism.

Smulders, Peter G. "Comments of Employee Absence/Attendance as a Dependent Variable in Organizational Research." *Journal of Applied Psychology*, 65 (June 1980), pp. 368–371. This article deals with three absentee issues: the forms of absence measures, the preferability of attendance measures over absence measures from both a theoretical and a practical point of view, and the lack of convincing logic for using an attendance model instead of an absence model.

Spencer, Daniel G., and Steers, Richard M. "The Influence of Personal Factors and

Perceived Work Experiences on Employee Turnover and Absenteeism." *Academy of Management Journal*, 23 (September 1980), pp. 567–572. An exploratory study of the relationship between two sets of determinants of withdrawal behavior, personal characteristics, and work-related experiences as they relate to turnover and absenteeism.

Steers, Richard M., and Rhodes, Susan R. "Major Influences on Employee Attendance: A Process Model." *Journal of Applied Psychology*, 63 (August 1978), pp. 391–407. A model of employee attendance based on a review of empirical research. It is suggested that attendance behavior is influenced by attendance motivation and the ability to attend work. Attendance motivation is a function of job satisfaction and various pressures to attend.

Stephens, T. A., Burroughs, W. A. "An Application of Operant Conditioning to Absenteeism in a Hospital Setting." *Journal of Applied Psychology* (August 1978), pp. 518–521. An experimental study of the impact of two financial reward systems on absenteeism of hospital employees. Both reward systems resulted in reduced absenteeism with no significant difference between them. Income level was not a relevant variable in the study.

Stumpf, Stephen A., and Dawley, Patricia Kelly. "Predicting Voluntary and Involuntary Turnover Using Absenteeism and Performance Indices." *Academy of Management Journal*, 24 (March 1981), pp. 148–163. A study relating several personal characteristics, absenteeism, and performance indices to voluntary and involuntary turnover for large city bank tellers.

Water, L. K., and Roach, Darrell. "Job Satisfaction, Behavioral Intention, and Absenteeism as Predictors of Turnover." *Personnel Psychology*, 32 (Summer 1979), pp. 393–397. A step-wise multiple regression of job satisfaction, intention to remain with the company, and frequency of absenteeism found that frequency of absenteeism and intent to remain added to the prediction of turnover but job satisfaction did not.

Weiss, William. "Smoking: Burning a Hole in the Balance Sheet." *Personnel Management*, 13 (May 1981), pp. 24–29. A study of the costs of smoking on American industry measured in terms of absenteeism, sickness, and losses in productivity supported by data from the United Kingdom.

Winkler, Donald. "The Effects of Sick-Leave Policy on Teacher Absenteeism." *Industrial and Labor Relations Review*, 33 (January 1980), pp. 232–240. A study of the effects of sick-leave policy on absenteeism in the public sector. Using short-term absenteeism and controlling for personal and job characteristics, the study found that three sick-leave policy variables were most influential: income protection plans that provide protection against loss of pay (result in higher short-form absenteeism), requiring proof of illness (leads to lower absenteeism), and requiring the employee to report to his or her supervisor (reduces absenteeism). Large staff size was positively related to short-term absenteeism.

Index

About the Authors

DAVID A. DILTS, Associate Professor of Labor Relations at Kansas State University, serves as arbitrator for several state labor boards and on the panels of the American Arbitration Association, Federal Mediation and Conciliation Service, and the National Mediation Board. He is the co-author, with Clarence R. Deitsch, of the widely used textbook, *Labor Relations,* and the author or coauthor of articles appearing in *Personnel Journal, Labor Law Journal,* and *Monthly Labor Review.*

CLARENCE R. DEITSCH, Professor of Economics at Ball State University, Muncie, Indiana, serves on the arbitration panels of the American Arbitration Association, Federal Mediation and Conciliation Service, and National Mediation Board, and as arbitrator for various state labor boards. He is co-author, with David A. Dilts, of *Labor Relations* and the author of articles appearing in *Arbitration Journal, Labor Law Journal,* and *Monthly Labor Review.*

ROBERT J. PAUL, Professor of Management at Kansas State University, is the author of more than fifty articles on manpower utilization. In addition to his many years of teaching experience, he has served as a consultant to industry and state government.

JAMES REDEKER is a partner in the law firm of Saul, Ewing, Remick & Saul of Philadelphia, Pennsylvania, Wilmington, Delaware, and New York, New York. He is chairman of the firm's labor department.